notes®

Guide to Literary Terms

by
Gail Rae
(M.A., Hunter College)
Department of English
McKee Vocational Technical High School
Staten Island, New York

Research & Education Association

What **MAXnotes®** *Will Do for You*

This book is intended to help you absorb the essential meaning and uses of the major literary terms and devices. Understanding literary terms and how they are used will help you gain a thorough understanding of a work of literature. This book has been designed to give you this understanding more quickly and effectively than any other study guide.

To help you in your studies, this book presents a concise definition, history, and example of every term. The entries are in alphabetical order to make finding a specific term simple. Cross-referencing of each entry aids in finding synonyms and similar definitions. Meaningful illustrations of important literary works are included for your enjoyment.

This **MAXnotes** guide also includes a special section to introduce you to the work of William Shakespeare. One of the most important literary figures in the Western world, Shakespeare's plays are mandatory reading for every student of literature. The section found in this book will make understanding and reading Shakespeare easier and more enjoyable.

The use of this study guide will save you hours of research and study time that would ordinarily be required to understand the terms and devices used in works of literature. Using this book will make you better prepared for classroom discussions, homework, and exams.

The **MAXnotes** will take your grades "to the max."

Dr. Max Fogiel
Program Director

Contents

Introduction

How to Use This Book

This book is intended to help you absorb the essential terms and devices used by writers and poets in their works. By understanding these literary terms, you will gain a more thorough understanding of the work you are reading.

This book has been designed to guide you to the terms you are looking for quickly and effectively. The use of this study guide will save you hours of preparation time that would ordinarily be required to arrive at a complete grasp of a work of literature.

For best results, this book should be used as a companion when studying a work of literature. By identifying and understanding the literary devices used by authors, your performance on exams, homework, and in classroom discussions will improve greatly.

About This Book

The entries are presented in alphabetical order. Each entry includes a definition; a history of the term's usage and its origin; an example of the term's use (if applicable); and specific references to texts in which the term has been used (if applicable).

Illustrations have been included to enhance your enjoyment while studying.

A special section on Shakespearean language has been included to introduce readers to the often-confusing terminology and sentence structure found in his works. Topics covered include the life and work of William Shakespeare, his use of sentences, words, wordplay, and dramatic verse.

Finally, a bibliography can be found at the end of the book to point you in the right direction for any further study you may need.

The *MAXNotes Guide to Literary Terms* provides insightful explanations, examples, and references to any literary term you may encounter. Using this book will dramatically raise your classroom and reading performance!

Example of an Entry

Oxymoron - a figure of speech in which two contradictory words or phrases are combined to produce a rhetorical effect by means of a concise paradox.

The term comes from the Greek *oxumoros*, meaning "pointedly foolish," which was formed by combining *oxus*, meaning "sharp," and *moros*, meaning "foolish."

An example is the word sophomore, which is a combination of two Greek words: "sophos," which means wise, and "moros," which means foolish.

The use of oxymoron is a common poetic device. In Shakespeare's *Sonnet 142*, the speaker declares:

"Love is my sin, and thy dear virtue hate."

Line 1

see: *antithesis, paradox*

SECTION TWO

Dictionary of Literary Terms

(the) Absurd - an avant-garde style in which structure, plot, and characterization are disregarded or garbled in order to stress the lack of logic in nature and man's isolation in a universe which has no meaning or value.

The term is derived from the Latin *absurdus,* formed from *ab* and *surdus,* meaning "deaf" and "stupid". Albert Camus used the word in discussing his concept of existentialism, the philosophy that the individual is responsible for whatever decisions (s)he makes according to the doctrine of free will, but that (s)he makes those decisions without knowing what is right or wrong, as demonstrated in his novel, *The Stranger.* In this novel, the protagonist, Meursault, commits a murder without seeming to realize either the seriousness or the consequences of such an act; there was neither an evaluation of the act before it was committed nor remorse for having done "wrong" after the fact. Living this way was considered absurd or senseless, illogical, and contrary to common sense.

Franz Kafka's *Metamorphosis* is an example of an absurdist short story, in which a man wakes one day having been mysteriously transformed into an insect. The term is usually used to indicate the Theater of the Absurd, a phrase invented by Martin Esslin in 1961 to refer to the plays of such 1950s dramatists as Eugéne Ionesco, Edward Albee, Jean Genet, Harold Pinter, and Samuel Beckett.

From Camus's *The Stranger*

Aesthetics (also spelled esthetics) - means the study of the emotions and the mind in relation to their sense of beauty in literature and other fine arts, but separately from moral, social, political, practical, or economic considerations. This area of study is concerned with the appreciation and criticism of what is considered beautiful or ugly. It is sometimes referred to as "art for art's sake."

The word comes from the Greek *aisthetikos*, meaning "perceptive," and was derived from *aisthanesthai*, which means "to feel" or "to perceive."

The term was introduced in 1753 by the German philosopher Alexander Gottlieb Baumgarent, but the study of the nature of beauty had been pursued for centuries, certainly since the time of Plato. The later Nineteenth Century saw the blossoming of the aesthetic movement in England. In the conclusion to *The Renaissance* (1873), a seminal work in the articulation of aesthetic theory, Walter Pater writes, "For art comes to you proposing frankly to give nothing but the highest quality to your moments as they pass, and simply for those moments' sake." Other major proponents of the aesthetic included John Ruskin and Oscar Wilde.

Affective fallacy - the error of judging a literary work by its emotional effect upon readers or a confusion between the work itself and its results.

The term comes from combining two words: affective, which means pertaining to emotional effects or natures, and fallacy, which means false or mistaken idea.

Affect was a Middle English word taken from the Middle French *affaire*, meaning "to influence;" *affaire* was derived from the Latin *afficere*, which was formed by joining *ab* and *facere*, meaning "to do." Fallacy is from the Latin *fallacia*, which was derived from *fallac-* or *fallax*, meaning "deceitful." These terms were originally from *fallere*, meaning "to deceive."

In essence, avoidance of the affective fallacy demonstrates an attempt to create objective literary criticism, in which the critic is

concerned with describing the rhetorical composition of a work—
how it functions — rather than with describing the impact of a work
— what it does — on the reader.

see: *catharsis*

Allegory - an extended metaphor in which a person, abstract idea,
or event stands for itself and for something else. It usually involves moral or spiritual concepts which are more significant
than the actual narrative.

The term is from the Greek *allegoria,* a joining of two other Greek
words: *allos,* meaning "other", and *agoreuein,* meaning "to speak."

The most famous allegory in English is Bunyan's *The Pilgrim's
Progress* (1678) which describes the adventures of the human soul
as if it were on a journey. Parts of Dante's *Divine Comedy* (1310–
1314) are also allegorical. George Orwell's *Animal Farm* (1946) is
a political allegory in which the story of the revolution of the animals on an English farm stands as a critique of both the capitalist
democracies of the west and the totalitarian regime that had grown
out of the communist revolution in Russia.

see: *fable, morality play, myth, parable, satire*

Alliteration (sometimes called initial rhyme) - common in poetry
and occasionally in prose, this is the repetition of an initial
sound in two or more words of a phrase, line, or sentence. It is
usually a consonant and marks the stressed syllables in a line
of poetry or prose. Alliteration may be considered ornamen-
tal or as a decoration which appeals to the sense of hearing.

The word comes from the Latin *ad literam,* which means "according to the letter."

This device was consistently used in Old English poetry, but
fell out of favor in the Middle Ages. Now it is used to emphasize
meaning and is especially effective in oratory. It is characteristic of
Anglo-Saxon poetry, as in *Beowulf,* and is still used by modern poets
in nonsense verse, tongue twisters, and jingles.

In *A Midsummer Night's Dream*, Shakespeare makes satirical use of alliteration in order to demonstrate the artisan-acting troupe's lack of poetic skill. In the play within the play, *Pyramus and Thisbe*, Quince says as prologue:

> Whereat, with blade, with bloody blameful blade,
> He bravely broached his boiling bloody breast.
>
> Act V, scene i : lines 155 – 156

Allusion - a reference, usually brief, often casual, occasionally indirect, to a person , event, or condition thought to be familiar (but sometimes actually obscure or unknown) to the reader. This holds true especially for the characters and events of mythology, legends, and history. Association is an essential part of allusion. The purpose of allusion is to bring a world of experience outside the limitations of a statement to the reader.

The term comes from Latin *alludere*, which means "to play with," "jest," or "refer to."

John Milton uses allusion in *Paradise Lost:*

> ...; and what resounds
> In fable or romance of Uther's son
> Begirt with British and Armoric knights;
> And all who since, baptized or infidel
> Jousted in Aspramont or Montalban,
> Damask, or Marocco, or Trebisond,
> Or whom Biserta sent from Afric shore
> When Charlemain with all his peerage fell
> By Fontarabbia.
>
> Book 1 : lines 479 – 587

In *The Merchant of Venice*, when Shylock seeks to compliment Portia for her agreeing that Bassanio must keep his bargain, Shakespeare has Shylock use the biblical allusion:

> A Daniel come to judgment! Yea, a Daniel.
>
> Act IV, scene i : line 221

From Milton's *Paradise Lost*

Ambiguity - a doubtfulness or uncertainty about the intention or meaning of something. It usually refers to a statement that is subject to more than one interpretation. The term is used for words that suggest two or more appropriate meanings or that convey both a basic meaning and complex overtones of that meaning. Sometimes, authors make deliberate choices of words that simultaneously cause several different streams of thought in the reader's mind. Ambiguity is also used to mean confusion between the denotation and connotation of a literary work. A simple kind of ambiguity is the use of homophones to promote a multiplicity of possible meanings. In Sonnet 135, Shakespeare puns on the word "Will," invoking its sense as one's wish, as well as its sense as a nickname for "William": "whoever hath her wish, thou hast thy Will" (line 1).

The word is derived from the Latin *ambiguus*, which means "doubtful," and was formed from *ambigere*—a combination of *amb*, meaning "both ways," and *agere*, meaning "drive."

see: *allusion, connotation*

Anachronism - an error in chronology, or placing an event, person, item, or language expression in the wrong period.

The term is originally from the Greek *anakhronismos* formed by combining *ana*, which means "back or backwards," and *khronos*, which means "time."

In Shakespeare's *Julius Caesar*, an anachronism is used:

> Brutus: Peace! count the clock.
> Cassius: The clock has stricken three.
>
> Act II, scene i : lines 193 – 194

There were no clocks during Roman times, and the striking clock was not invented until 1,400 years after Caesar's death.

Contemporary theater often uses anachronisms, such as when one of Shakespeare's plays is performed in modern-day clothing.

Analogy - the relationship of similarity between two or more enti-
ties or a partial similarity on which a comparison is based. An
example is the classic analogy between the heart and a pump.
In argumentation and persuasion, analogy is often used as a
form of reasoning in which one thing is compared to or contrasted with another in certain respects, based on the known
similarity or dissimilarity in other respects. Analogy is often
used to paint vivid word pictures.

The term comes from the Greek *analogia*, meaning "proportion."

In *Gulliver's Travels*, Jonathan Swift describes the societies of
the Lilliputians and the Brobdingrags in such a way as to make their
characteristics and weaknesses analogous to human society.

see: *metaphor, simile*

Antagonist - the character who strives against another main
character. This character opposes the hero or protagonist in
drama. The term is also used to describe one who contends
with or opposes another in a fight, conflict, or battle of wills.
In literature, this is the principal opponent or foil of the main
character and is considered the villain unless the protagonist
is a villain; in that case, the antagonist is the hero.

The word is derived from the Greek *antagonistes*, which means
"rival" and was formed from the combining of *anti*, meaning
"against," and *agon*, meaning a "contest."

Shakespeare's plays provide apt examples of antagonists: his
Macduff in *Macbeth* is an antagonist and the hero, since the protagonist—Macbeth—is a villain; Laertes and Claudius are the
antagonists of Hamlet in the play of the same name; Iago is
Othello's antagonist in *Othello*. Also, the antagonist does not have
to be another person. In Jack London's story "To Build a Fire," the
antagonist is the bitterly cold weather.

see: *protagonist*

From Swift's *Gulliver's Travels*

Anticlimax - a drop, often sudden and unexpected, from a dignified or important idea or situation to a trivial one or a descent from something sublime to something ridiculous. In fiction and drama, this refers to action which is disappointing in contrast to the previous moment of intense interest or anything which follows the climax. The effect may be comic and is often intended to be. According to Samuel Johnson, who first recorded the word, it is "A sentence in which the last part expresses something lower than the first."

The term comes from the combination of two Greek words: *anti*, which means "against" or "the reverse of," and *klimax*, which means "a ladder" and was derived from *klinein* meaning "to slope."

An example of an anticlimax is when the indigent protagonist finds a great amount of money for which (s)he has been intently searching and does nothing with it.

see: *climax*

Antithesis - contrary ideas expressed in a balanced sentence. It is the juxtaposition of two words, phrases, clauses, or sentences contrasted or opposed in meaning in such a way as to give emphasis to their contrasting ideas and give the effect of balance. This is a device often used in rhetoric.

The word comes from the Greek *anti*, meaning "against," and *tithenai*, which means "to place" or "to set against."

In Milton's *Paradise Lost* (1667), Adam and Eve are described using antitheses:

> For contemplation he and valour formed,
> For softness she and sweet attractive grace;
> He for God only, she for God in him.
>
> Book V, lines 297 – 299

see: *epigram, figure of speech, oxymoron*

Aphorism - a brief, pithy, usually concise statement or observation of a doctrine, principle, truth, or sentiment. Aphorisms are usually not anonymous.

The word comes from the Greek *aphorizein,* which means "to mark off by boundaries" and was formed by combining *apo,* meaning "from," and *horos,* meaning "a limit." The term was first used by Hippocrates.

An example of an aphorism is Benjamin Franklin's

> Early to bed
> and early to rise,
> makes a man
> healthy, wealthy, and wise.

see: *epigram, proverb*

Apocalyptic - connected with revelation. The term is also used to describe literature that provides a prophecy or revelation. In contemporary usage, this refers to any literary selection that reveals and predicts the future. Usually, the term is used to refer to the coming of the end of the world and the expected final battle between good and evil.

The word is from the Greek *apokalupsis,* which means "unveiling," and was originally derived from *kaluptein,* meaning "to cover."

It is used as the title of the last book in The New Testament of the Bible: The Apocalypse or the Revelation of St. John the Divine. The final two books of *Paradise Lost* are apocalyptic, as the archangel Michael shows Adam how human history will climax in the final judgement of God.

Apology - a defense and justification for some belief, doctrine, piece of writing, cause, or action without any admission of blame with which we contemporarily associate the word. In the Eighteenth Century, the word came to be used loosely almost as a synonym for autobiography without any suggestion of justifying or defending the writer's ideas or conduct.

The term comes from the Greek *apologia*, meaning defense. This Greek word was formed by joining *apo*, which means away, and *logia*, which means speaking.

Plato recorded Socrates's *Apologia* in the Fourth Century B.C. At the end of Geoffrey Chaucer's *Canterbury Tales*, there is a retraction or apology for his work; in this case, apology means both an explanation and an expression of regret.

Arbitrary - lacking any natural basis or substantial justification; determined by whim with little thought.

This term was originally from the Latin *arbitrari*, derived from *arbitr-* or *arbiter*, meaning "to witness."

Mark Twain's *Huckleberry Finn* contains many instances of Huck's arbitrary choice of actions, such as when he chose not to accept the Widow Douglas's home as his own, preferring to run away instead or, as Huck stated in the second paragraph of the novel, " . . . when I couldn't stand it no longer I lit out."

Archetype (also called prototype) - the original model or pattern from which copies are made or from which something develops. It is also a symbol, theme, setting, or character that is thought to have some universal meaning and recurs in different times and places in myth, literature, folklore, dreams, and rituals.

The term is from the Greek *archetupon*, meaning "pattern" or "model."

The psychologist Carl Jung identified the archetype in the collective unconscious of mankind: the ideas or modes of thought derived from the experiences of a race—such as birth, death, love, family life, struggles—inherited in the subconscious of an individual from ancestors and expressed in myths, dreams, and literature.

Plato was the first philosopher to use archetypes, especially those of beauty, truth, and goodness. Sophocles used the archetypes of blindness, patricide, incest, and fratricide. Hawthorne and

Melville focused on the archetypes of sin, retribution, and death in their works (*The Scarlet Letter* and *Billy Budd*, respectively). The Greek Myth of Pandora introduces the archetype of the mischievous woman, exemplified by Madame Merle in James's *Portrait of a Lady* (1881).

see: *folklore, imagery, literature, myth.*

Ballad - a short, narrative folk song that fixes on the most dramatic part of a story, moving to its conclusion by the means of dialogue and a series of incidences. It represents a type of literary and musical development across Europe in the late Middle Ages and tends to have a tight dramatic structure that sometimes omits all preliminary material, all exposition and description, even all motivation, to focus on the climactic scene. The narrator is impersonal and the listener or reader is left to supply the antecedent material. Folk ballads are transmitted orally, and therefore, subject to continual change, although most seem to be domestic, simple, stanzad, rhymed, and use language and action which are stylized. Clichés and conventionalized conduct are typical in ballads which are still common in northern Greece, parts of the central Balkans, and Sicily. Originally, the term signified a song accompanied by a dance. Later, it came to mean a narrative poem with short stanzas designed for singing or oral recitation. There are four types of ballads:

1. folk ballad which is derived from the medieval oral traditions
2. literary ballad which is a deliberate attempt by its author to capture the charm of the folk ballad
3. broadside ballad which proliferated in the Eighteenth Century, sold for a penny: printed on sheets of paper called "broadside," they included suggestions for the tune to which they should be sung
4. a sentimental tune with melodramatic lyrics, popular in the Nineteenth and Twentieth Centuries.

The word comes from the Old French *ballade*, which derived from the Provençal *ballada*. This originated from the Low Latin *ballare*, which means "to dance."

An example of a ballad is "Bill," which has been sung by sailors for decades:

> He lay dead on the cluttered deck and stared at the cold skies,
> With never a friend to mourn for him nor a hand to close his eyes:
> "Bill, he's dead," was all they said; "he's dead, 'n' there he lies."
> The mate came forward at seven bells and spat across the rail:
> "Just lash him up wi' some holystone in a clout o' rotten sail,
> "'N', rot ye, get a gait on ye, ye're slower'n a bloody snail!"
> When the rising moon was a copper disc and the sea was a strip of steel,
> We dumped him down to the swaying weeds ten fathom beneath the keel.
> "It's rough about Bill," the fo'c's'le said, "we'll have to stand his wheel."

see: *folklore*

Bard - one of an ancient Celtic order of versifiers, especially one who was highly trained as a composer, singer, and harpist who recited heroic and adventurous poems. This type of versifier was the oral historian, political critic, eulogizer, and entertainer of his society. Poems passed from bard to bard orally with each bard adding some personal embroidery. Their memorization was aided by certain formulas such as fixed phrases and repeated verses or groups of verses. The most prominent bards lived in medieval and post-medieval Wales and Ireland, many as residents in wealthy homes, others as itinerants. In Wales, bards were often nobles and formed guilds to set standards for writing and reciting. They were repeatedly outlawed by the English as politically inciting, causing their gradual extinction. The word is still used to describe a recognized singer at the Welsh musical festival, Eisteddfod.

The word was taken from the Gaelic and Irish *bard* or *bardh*, approximately meaning "poet," but specifically meaning the type of poet described above.

Now the word is a synonym for poet as in "Shakespeare, the Bard of Avon."

Bibliography - a list of readings on a particular subject. Included in the list are authors, titles, editions, and dates and places of publication. Bibliographies can be divided into two categories: the enumerative, which lists alphabetically or chronologically, and the critical, which lists evaluations or comparisons of the items. In library science, however, the term means the study of the history, physical description, and classification of books, graphic materials, etc.

The word is from the Greek *bibliographia*, meaning "the writing of books" and was used to describe the writing or copying of books until the mid-Eighteenth Century.

An example of a bibliography may be found at the end of this book.

Black comedy - Often considered perverted and morbid, black comedy depicts situations normally thought of as tragic or grave as humorous. Specifically, it displays marked disillusionment and depicts humans without convictions and with little hope. The term is also used to describe theater dealing with sinister or disturbing subjects handled lightly in an attempt to offend and shock, as is common in Theater of the Absurd.

Black is from the Middle English *blak* derived from the Old English *blaec*, which is probably the same as the Latin *flagrare*, meaning "to burn." Comedy is derived from the Latin *comoedia* which, in turn, was from the Greek *komoidia* formed by joining *komos*, meaning "revel," and, *aidein*, meaning "to sing."

Kurt Vonnegut, Jr. is a Twentieth-Century novelist whose works, including *Cat's Cradle* and *Slaughterhouse-Five* are filled with black comedy. There are representatives of the genre in Twentieth Century drama such as Beckett's *Waiting for Godot*.

see: *absurd*

Blank verse (also called unrhymed iambic pentameter) - unrhymed lines of ten syllables each with the even-numbered syllables bearing the accents. Blank verse is considered best for dramatic verse in English since it is the verse form closest to the rhythms of everyday English speech and has been the dominant verse form of English drama and narrative poetry since the mid-Sixteenth Century. Such verse is blank in rhyme only, having a definite meter, although variations in meter are sometimes used. As Milton explained in his 1667 preface to *Paradise Lost:*

> The Measure is English Heroic Verse without Rime, as that of Homer in Greek, and of Virgil in Latin; Rime being no necessary Adjunct or true Ornament of Poem or good Verse, in larger Works especially, but the Invention of a barbarous Age, to set off wretched matter and lame Meeter.

The term is originally from the French *blanc*, meaning "white"— in the sense of "left white" or "requiring something to be filled in."

The term was first used by the Earl of Surrey, Henry Howard, in 1540 in his translation of Books II and III of *The Aeneid* of Virgil, but previously had been adapted by Italian Renaissance writers from classical sources. It was used a great deal for reflective and narrative poems until the late Seventeenth Century. In the latter Nineteenth Century, the English romantic poets—Wordsworth, Shelley, and Keats—made use of blank verse. Later yet, the English poets, Robert Browning and Lord Tennyson, and the American poets, Robinson and Frost, employed it for less lofty themes, leading its use to become more colloquial in tone.

In Shakespeare's *A Midsummer Night's Dream*, Theseus's speech to Hippolyta explaining the lovers' rearrangement of couples is written in blank verse:

> The poet's eye, in a fine frenzy rolling,
> Doth glance from heaven to earth,
> from earth to heaven;
> And, as imagination bodies forth
> The forms of things unknown, the poet's pen
> Turns them to shapes and gives to airy nothing
> A local habitation and a name.

Act V, scene i : lines 12 – 17

From Kafka's *Metamorphosis*

Bombast - originally, cotton or any soft material used for padding to produce clothes in the fashion of the Sixteenth Century. It has come to mean a highflown unnatural style, rather inflated and insincere, pretentious, ranting, and using extravagant language. Also, it can denote extravagance at the expense of content.

The word is from the Greek *bombux*, meaning "silkworm" or "silk," and the Latin *bombyx*, meaning "silkworm," "something made of silk, any fine fiber, or cotton." Both were used to form the Old French *bombace*, meaning "cotton."

In Shakespeare's *Othello*, Iago uses the word in complaining to Roderigo about Othello:

> But he, as loving of his own pride and purposes,
> Evades them with a bombast circumstance
> Horribly stuff'd with epithets of war;
> And, in conclusion,
> Nonsuits my mediators.
>
> Act I, scene i : lines 13 – 17

see: *hyperbole*

Canon - a standard of judgment or a criterion. It is also an approved list of books belonging in the Christian Bible, in addition to being the accepted list of any given order, and the list of books accepted as Scripture. The term is increasingly used to refer to those works of literature that have come to be considered standard in any anthology or course of study. In addition, it refers to the works of an author which are accepted as genuine, such as the Chaucer Canon.

The term is derived from the Middle French *canon*, which was adapted from the Italian *cannone*, meaning "large tube." This definition evolved from the Latin *canna*, which meant "cane or reed." Common usage eventually led to the term being defined as a straight rod or bar, a carpenter's rule, or a standard of excellence. Greek authors were known as *kanones* or "models of excellence."

Melville's canon consists of *Moby-Dick* and *Billy Budd*.

Canto - one of the main or larger divisions of a long poem. It is also used to denote a singing or chanting section of a poem, or a subdivision of an epic or narrative (comparable to a chapter in a novel).

The word is taken from the Italian, which originally took it from the Latin *cantus,* meaning "song."

Dante's *The Divine Comedy* is divided into cantos.

Catharsis - any emotional discharge which brings about a moral or spiritual renewal or welcome relief from tension and anxiety. The usual intent is for an audience to leave feeling this relief from tension or anxiety after having viewed a play.

The word comes from the Greek *katharis,* meaning "cleansing, or purification." This evolved from *kathairo,* which means I cleanse, and *katharos,* which means "pure or clean."

Catharsis was referred to by Aristotle (384 – 322 B.C.) in his *Poetics:*

> Tragedy, then, is an imitation of an action that is serious, complete, and of a certain magnitude; . . . through pity and fear effecting the proper purgation of these emotions.
>
> Book 6 : 2

Character - an aggregate of traits and features that form the nature of some person or animal. It also refers to moral qualities and ethical standards and principles. In literature, character refers to a person represented in a story, novel, play, etc.

The word is from the Greek *kharakter,* meaning "stamp," and *kharassein,* meaning "to engrave." Originally, the Greek philosopher Theophrastus (372 – 287 B.C.), a pupil of Aristotle's, used it in his book *Characters* which contained short prose sketches of different types of people molded to a pattern which served as a model for some Seventeenth-Century writers. In Seventeenth and Eighteenth-century England, a character was a formal sketch or descriptive analysis of a particular virtue or vice as represented in a person, what is now more often called a character sketch.

From Shakespeare's *Othello*

Chaucer wrote character sketches in the General Prologue to his *The Canterbury Tales.*

Characterization - the creation of the image of imaginary persons in drama, narrative poetry, the novel, and the short story. Characterization generates plot and is revealed by actions, speech, thoughts, physical appearance, and the other characters' thoughts or words about him.

The etymology and derivation of the word are the same as those for character.

In Mark Twain's *Huckleberry Finn,* Huck's use of dialect, running away, his guardian's feelings about him, and Jim's response to him all comprise Twain's characterization of his protagonist.

see: *allegory, fable, plot, thesis*

Chorus - a group of singers distinct from the principal performers in a dramatic or musical performance and, also, the song or refrain that they sing.

The word comes from the Greek *choros,* meaning "a company of dancers or singers," or "a group of persons singing in unison."

In ancient Greece, a chorus was a group of male singers and dancers who participated in religious festivals and dramatic performances as actors, commenting on the deeds of the characters and interpreting the significance of events within the play for the audience.

In Aeschylus's works, the chorus takes part in the action of the play, while in Sophocles's, the chorus comments on the action. In Euripides's works, the chorus is lyrical. During the Elizabethan era, a single actor recited both the prologue and the epilogue, and sometimes commented in-between acts to interpret the significance of events, as in Shakespeare's *Henry V,* in which The Chorus is a character. Contemporarily, the playwrights T. S. Eliot and Brecht used choruses in their *Murder in the Cathedral* (1935) and *The Caucasian Chalk Circle* (1948), respectively.

Chronicle (also called history) - a detailed and continuous record of events, usually a systematic account or narration of events that contain little or no interpretation or analysis.

The word is from the Greek *khronos*, meaning "time," and *khronik*, meaning "annals."

Chronicles were used as a form of history from Roman times until the early 1600s when they were largely replaced by biographies, autobiographies, memoirs, diaries, logs, travel books, and narratives of sea voyages and exploration.

Shakespeare adapted Holinshed's *Chronicles of England, Scotland, and Ireland* (1577) for his history plays, such as *Henry V.*

Climax - the moment in a play, novel, short story, or narrative poem at which the crisis comes to its point of greatest intensity and is resolved. It is also the peak of emotional response from a reader or spectator, and it usually represents the turning point in the action. Additionally, the term is used for the arrangement of words, clauses, or sentences in order of their importance, the least forcible coming first and the others rising in power until the last or, simply, the last term of the arrangement. Climax also means a culmination.

The word comes from the Greek *klimax*, meaning "a ladder," and *klinein*, meaning "to slope, or slant."

The climax of *Beowulf* is when Beowulf slays the mother of the monster, Grendel. Hardy's *Tess of the D'urbervilles* (1891) climaxes when Tess murders Alec D'urberville, who has harassed and tormented her throughout the novel.

see: *anticlimax, denouement*

Closure - the sense of completion or resolution at the end of a literary work or part of a work. In literary criticism, it is the reduction of a work's meanings to a single and complete sense that excludes the claims of other interpretations.

The term came from Middle English, which took it from Middle French, and was originally from the Latin *clausura,* meaning "to close."

An example of closure is the Finale in George Eliot's *Middlemarch* in which the author explains what happened to each of the characters in the novel.

Colloquialism - a word or phrase used in an easy, informal style of writing or speaking. It is usually more appropriate in speech than formal writing. Colloquialisms appear often in literature since they provide a sense of actual conversation and use the pronunciation, grammar, and vocabulary of everyday speech.

The word is taken from the Latin *colloqui,* which is a joining of *com,* meaning "with or together," and *loqui,* meaning "to speak" and "conversation."

Mark Twain makes use of colloquialisms in his *Huckleberry Finn,* such as in the opening line of the story:

> "You don't know about me without you have read a book by the name of *The Adventures of Tom Sawyer,* but that ain't no matter."

see: *dialogue, idiom*

Comedy - a ludicrous and amusing event or series of events designed to provide enjoyment and produce smiles or laughter usually written in a light, familiar, bantering, or satirical style. Comedy is the opposite of tragedy. Dramatic comedy begins in difficulty and rapidly involves its characters in amusing situations and ends happily, but not all comedies are humorous and lighthearted. It differs from burlesque and farce in that comedy has a more closely knit plot, more sensible and intelligent dialogue, and more plausible characterization. Often comedy assures its desired effect by stressing some oddity or incongruity of character, speech, or action—perhaps by

From the Beowulf Poet's *Beowulf*

caricature or exaggeration. There are many different kinds of comedy with the most usual being:

1. the comedy of humors in which characters' actions are controlled by some whim or humor,
2. the comedy of manners which involves the conventions or manners of artificial and sophisticated society, and
3. the comedy of intrigue or situation which depends more on plot than characterization.

There are also topical, romantic, satirical, and verbal wit comedies.

The word comes from the French *comedie* which was derived from the Greco-Latin *comoedia* which was formed by combining *komos*, meaning "to revel," and *aeidein*, meaning "to sing."

In the Middle Ages, comedy referred to narrative poems that ended happily, such as Dante's *Divine Comedy* (1320). Prior to that, comedy may be traced as far back as Aristophanes, the Fifth Century B.C. Greek playwright.

An example of contemporary comedy comes from Faye Kellerman's *The Quality of Mercy*:

> "Aye, a strong neck I have. Yet it is neither as long nor graceful as thine—" He corrected himself. "As *yours*. As far as the head is concerned, I've been told I have a head for words, yet not much of one for numbers and none for science and languages, as you have. So as far as heads go, you are heads above me. Which explains why your neck is longer than mine."

see: *black comedy, comic relief, farce*

Comic relief (also called episode and interlude) - a humorous scene, incident, or remark occurring in the midst of a serious or tragic literary selection and deliberately designed to relieve emotional intensity and simultaneously to heighten, increase, and highlight the seriousness or tragedy of the action. Apart from being a simple diversion, though, comic relief normally plays some part in advancing the action of drama.

The phrase comes from two words: the first, comic, has the same etymology as that of comedy which is discussed above; relief may be traced from Middle English, back to Middle French, and originally to the Old French *relever*, meaning "to relieve."

Since the Sixteenth Century, tragedians have almost universally used comic relief, as in Shakespeare's drunken porter in *Macbeth*:

> Here's a knocking indeed! If a man were porter of hell gate, he should have old turning the key. Knock, knock, knock! Who's there, i' the name of Belzebub? Here's a farmer that hanged himself on the expectation of plenty. Come in time! Have napkins enow about you; here you'll sweat for't. Knock, knock! Who's there, in the other devil's name? Faith, here's an equivocator, that could swear in both the scales against either scale; who committed treason enough for God's sake, yet could not equivocate to heaven. O, come in, equivocator! Knock, knock, knock! Who's there? Faith, here's an English tailor come hither for stealing out of a French hose. Come in, tailor. Here you may roast your goose. Knock, knock! Never at quiet! What are you? But this place is too cold for hell. I'll devil-porter it no further. I had thought to have let in some of all professions that go the primrose way to the everlasting bonfire. Anon, anon! I pray you remember the porter.
>
> Act II, scene iii : lines 1 – 19

see: *black comedy, comedy, farce, subplot*

Conceit - describing a person or idea by use of an analogy which often seems farfetched but proves surprisingly apt in pointing out parallels between the two being compared. A conceit may be considered an extravagant metaphor making an analogy between totally dissimilar things.

From Dante's *Divine Comedy*

The word comes from the Latin *concipere* or *conceptum*, which was formed by combining *con*, meaning "with or together," and *capere*, meaning "to take." Originally, the word was used to mean "concept or idea."

The term has been used since Petrarch (1304 – 1374). The fanciful images and startling comparisons frequently used in Elizabethan poetry are conceits. In his sonnets, Shakespeare used conceits such as:

> "So you are to my thoughts as food to life, or as sweet-season'd showers are to the ground."

> LXXV : lines 1-2

see: *analogy, hyperbole, metaphor, oxymoron, paradox*

Connotation - suggestions and associations which surround a word as opposed to its bare, literal meaning. It is the opposite of denotation. Literature uses connotation; science and philosophy use denotation. Connotation refers to qualities, attributes, and characteristics implied or suggested by the word and depends upon the context in which the word is used. Metaphors depend a great deal on connotation. Connotations often elicit emotional responses from the reader.

The word is from the Latin *connotare*, meaning "to mark together."

In his love poetry, John Donne often uses the word "die" which in the Renaissance had a sexual connotation, such as in these lines from "The Canonization:"

> "We die and rise the same and prove mysterious by this love."

see: *context, device, figure of speech, metaphor*

Content (also called subject matter or substance) - things or substances in an enclosed space, such as topics, ideas, statements, or facts in a book, document, letter, etc. This is true not only of forms, but also thought, feeling, attitude, and intention as conveyed by the words and their arrangement—especially what is said, rather than how it is said, in literature and in poetry.

The word is taken directly from the Latin *continere*, meaning "to contain."

Context - the part of a written (or spoken) statement which leads up to, follows, and specifies the meaning of that statement. The context of a group of words is nearly always very intimately connected as to throw light upon not only the meaning of individual words, but also the sense and purpose of an entire work.

The term is taken from the Latin *contextus* which is from *contexere*, meaning "to weave together."

Understanding the context in which a work of literature was produced often leads to a deeper understanding of the work itself; for instance, understanding the social and economic position of women in the early Nineteenth Century can provide a greater insight into the characterizations of women in Jane Austen's novels.

Couplet - a pair of successive lines of verse, especially a pair that rhymes, that are of the same metrical length, and form a single unit. The term is also used for lines that express a complete thought or form a separate stanza. Couplets are usually written in decasyllabic lines. A closed couplet is one that is logically and grammatically complete.

The word comes from the French diminutive of *couple* which was derived from the Latin *copula*, meaning "a band or bond."

The form was first used by Chaucer in the Fourteenth Century. Tudor and Jacobean poets and dramatists used it as a variation of blank verse and to round off a scene or act. The couplet eventually evolved into the heroic couplet, which was rhymed iambic pentameter and popular in the Seventeenth and Eighteenth Centuries. Nineteenth-Century Romantic poetry used the couplet, as do epigrams.

Shakespeare used this form in the concluding lines of his sonnets. Chaucer used it in his "Merchant's Tale" within *The Canterbury Tales*:

> Whilom ther was dwellynge in Lumbardye
> A worthy knyght, that born was of Pavye,
> In which he lyved in greet prosperitee;
> And sixty yeer a wyflees man was hee,
> And folwed ay his bodily delyt
> On wommen, ther as was his appetyt...

lines 1 – 6

see: *epigram, stanza, sonnet*

Denouement - refers to the outcome or result of a complex situation or sequence of events. It is the final outcome or unraveling of the main dramatic complications in a play, novel, or
other work of literature. In drama, the term is usually applied
to tragedies or to comedies with catastrophes in their plot. Denouement is usually the final scene or chapter in which any
necessary, and, as yet unmade, clarifications are made.

The word is taken directly from French and means literally
"untying." The French *nouer* is from the Latin *nodare* which was
derived from *nodus*, meaning "knot to untie."

An example of denouement is when, after Beowulf has once
again saved a group of villagers, this time from a dragon, the poet
writes of Beowulf's funeral and the grief of his followers (lines 3058 –
3182).

see: *anticlimax, climax, plot*

Device - a term used to describe any literary technique deliberately employed to achieve a specific effect such as: *in medias
res* in novels; parallelism in rhetoric; alliteration, simile, and
metaphor in poetry; soliloquy in drama; and hyperbole, paradox, and oxymoron in conceits.

The term is from the Middle English *devis* via Middle French
from the Old French *deviser*, meaning "to divide, regulate, or tell."

see: *alliteration, conceit, drama, figure of speech, hyperbole, in me-dias res, metaphor, novel, oxymoron, paradox, parallelism, poetry, rhetoric, simile, soliloquy*

Dialect - the language of a particular district, class, or group of persons. It encompasses the sounds, grammar, and diction employed by a specific people as distinguished from other persons either geographically or socially. Dialect, as a major technique of characterization, is the use by persons in a narrative of distinct varieties of language to indicate a person's social or geographical status, and is used by authors to give an illusion of reality to fictional characters. It is sometimes used to differentiate between characters.

The word is derived from the Greek *dialektos* which evolved from *dialegesthai*, meaning "to discourse."

Mark Twain used dialect in his *Huckleberry Finn* to differentiate between characters, such as when Huck and Jim are discussing Jim's freedom:

> Jim: "We's safe, Huck, we's safe! Jump up and crack yo' heels! Dat's de good ole Cairo at las', I jis knows it!"
>
> Huck: "I'll take the canoe and go see, Jim. It mightn't be, you know."
>
> Chapter XVI : The Rattlesnake-Skin Does Its Work

George Eliot also made use of dialect in her novels, such as *Silas Marner* and *Middlemarch*.

Dialogue - is a conversation, or a literary work in the form of a conversation, that is often used to reveal characters and to advance the plot. Also, the lines spoken by a character in a play, essay, story, or novel.

The word is derived from the Greek *dialogosa*, meaning "conversation." This Greek word evolved from *dialegesthai*, meaning "to discourse."

From Chaucer's *The Canterbury Tales*

Greek philosophers used dialogue as the best way to instruct their students.

In Shakespeare's *Romeo and Juliet,* Juliet's good night to Romeo is part of the dialogue:

Juliet: Tis almost morning: I would have
        thee gone:
And yet no further than a
        wanton's bird:
Who lets it hop a little from
        her hand,
Like a poor prisoner in his
        twisted gyves,
And with a silk thread plucks
        it back again,
so loving - jealous of his liberty.

Romeo: I would I were thy bird.

Juliet: Sweet, so would I:
Yet I should kill thee with
        much cherishing.
Good night, good night! Parting
        is such sweet sorrow,
That I shall say good night till
        it be morrow.

Act II, scene ii : lines 189-201

An example of a modern dialogue is the following from Margaret Truman's *Murder in Georgetown*:

"Joe, I'm so glad you're here."

"Yeah, me too. What's happened? Why did they do this to you? Have you been like this since you disappeared?"

She shook her head. "No, nothing like this. They brought me here and—"

"Who brought you here?"

"I don't know. They brought me here and I've been okay. They've treated me well. I've had good food and they even let me play the piano. They talk to me."

Digression - a passage or section of writing that departs from the central theme or basic plot, usually within the framework of the piece of writing rather than added at the end or prefaced at the beginning. It is used extensively in storytelling.

The term is taken from the Latin *digressus*, which was formed by combining *dis*, meaning "apart," and *gradi*, "to step."

Laurence Sterne famously used the digression throughout his work *Tristram Shandy* (1759) to produce a startling unconventional narrative form; the story begins with a description of the title character's conception, but the event of his birth is delayed for some 200 pages of asides and anecdotes.

Drama - a composition in prose or verse presenting, in pantomime and dialogue, a narrative involving conflict and usually designed for presentation on a stage. Aristotle called it "imitated human action." This type of composition needs a theater, actors, and an audience in order to be fully experienced; reading it is not enough. Sometimes, the word is used to mean a serious play.

The word is taken directly from the Greek *drama*, meaning "a deed or action of the stage." The Greek word evolved from the Greek term *dran*, meaning "to do" or "to act."

Drama arose from religious ceremonies, as opposed to comedy and tragedy's evolvement from themes in ceremonies such as fertility, life, death. Thespis of Sixth Century B.C. Attica was the first composer and soloist in tragedy. Aeschylus added a second actor to allow conflict and dialogue. Sophocles and Euripides added a third. Medieval drama largely evolved from the rites commemorating birth and the resurrection of Christ. During the Renaissance, we can see the beginning of drama as we know it: a picture of human life revealed in successive changes or events and told in dialogue and action for the entertainment and instruction of an audience. During the mid-Sixteenth Century, England was host to one of the greatest eras of world drama. It was during the Elizabethan/Jacobean Age that Shakespeare wrote his 38 plays.

According to the modern definition, any play (such as Beckett's *Waiting for Godot*) may be considered a drama.

see: *absurd, antagonist, dialogue, protagonist, satire, tragedy*

Elegy - a mournful, melancholy poem, especially a funeral song or lament for the dead or a personal, reflective poem.

The word comes from the Greek *elegeia* derived from *elegos*, meaning "mournful poem."

Elegies originated in Greek and Roman literature where they were used for various subjects such as death, war, or love and were distinguished for having a specific meter, rather than for their subject matter. Since the Sixteenth Century, modern poets characterized elegies not by the form, but by the content, which was invariably melancholy and centered on death.

The best known elegy in English is "Elegy Written in a Country Churchyard" by Thomas Gray (1751).

Ellipsis or ellipse - the omission of a word or words that a reader must supply for full understanding, or a mark or marks to indicate the omission or suppression of words, phrases, etc. This also means the omission in a sentence of one or more words needed to express the sense completely.

The word is taken from the Greek *elleipsis* derived from *elleipein*, meaning "to fall short" or "a deficiency."

Sometimes the words are omitted for compact expression, as in T. S. Eliot's use of ellipses in "The Wasteland":

> Elizabeth and Leicester
> Beating oars
> The stern was formed
> A gilded shell
> Red and gold
> The brisk swell
> Rippled both shores
> Southwest wind

> Carried down stream
> The peal of bells
> White towers

lines 279 – 289

Epic (sometimes called heroic poem) - a lengthy narrative poem
in which the action, characters, and language are on a heroic
level and the style is exalted and even majestic. Early epics
often stemmed from oral traditions. The major characteristics
of an epic are:

1. a setting remote in time and place
2. an objective, lofty, dignified style
3. a central incident or series of incidents dealing with legendary or traditional material
4. a theme involving universal human problems
5. a towering hero of great stature
6. superhuman strength of body, character, or mind
7. superhuman forces entering the action

The word is from the Greek *epikos* which was derived from
epos, meaning "word," "narrative," or "poem."

The ancient Greeks recited epics but sang lyric poetry. The epics summarized and expressed the nature or ideals of an entire na-
tion at a significant or crucial period of its history. The characteristics of the hero in an epic are national, rather than individual,
so that the exercise of those traits served to gratify the sense of
national pride. Epics may also synthesize the ideals of a great religious or cultural movement such as Dante's *The Divine Comedy*
did with medieval Christianity in the Fourteenth Century, or *Paradise Lost* written in 1667 by the Englishman John Milton to represent the ideals of Christian humanism. Usually, epics are the result
of a number of ballads or lays, or short ballads, gradually joined
together by poets or bards. An example is a thane beginning to com-
pose a lay about Beowulf in the epic poem of the same name:

> And sometimes a proud old soldier
> Who had heard songs of the ancient heroes
> And could sing them all through, story after story,

> Would weave a net of words for Beowulf's
> Victory tying the knot of his verses
> Smoothly, swiftly, into place with a poet's
> Quick skill, singing his new song aloud
> While he shaped it, and the old songs as well -
>
> lines 867 – 873

Homer's *The Iliad* and *The Odyssey*, and *The Aeneid* of Virgil are ancient epics. In modern writing, specific novels are referred to as epic, such as Melville's *Moby-Dick* and Steinbeck's *The Grapes of Wrath*.

Epigram - a witty, ingenious, and pointed saying that is tersely expressed.

The term is from the Greek *epigramma*, meaning "an inscription," and was formed by combining *epi*, meaning "upon," and *gramma*, meaning "a writing," or *graphein*, meaning "to write."

Originally, it meant an inscription or epitaph, usually in verse, on a building, tomb, or coin. Then it came to mean a short poem ending in a witty or ingenious turn of thought.

Pope included an epigram in his "Essay on Criticism":

> Be not the first by whom the new are tried,
> Nor yet the last to lay the old aside.
>
> lines 335 – 336

see: *antithesis, aphorism, epithet, proverb*

Epilogue - a concluding part added to such a literary work as a novel, play, or long poem. It is the opposite of a prologue. Sometimes, the word is used to refer to the moral of a fable. Often, we see it as a speech by one of the actors at the end of a play asking for the indulgence of the critics and audience.

The word comes from the Greek *epilogos*, meaning "conclusion," and was formed by combining *epi*, meaning "upon," and *legein*, meaning "to speak."

Shakespeare used an epilogue at the end of his *A Midsummer Night's Dream:*

> If we shadows have offended,
> Think but this and all is mended:
> That you have but slumbered here
> While these visions did appear.
> And this weak and idle theme,
> No more yielding but a dream,
> Gentles, do not reprehend.
> If you pardon, we will mend.
> And, as I am an honest Puck,
> If we have unearned luck
> Now to 'scape the serpent's tongue,
> We will make amends ere long.
> Else the Puck a liar call.
> So good night unto you all.
> Give me your hands, if we be friends,
> And Robin shall restore amends.
>
> Act V, scene i : lines 440 – 455

Epithet - an adjective which expresses a quality or attribute considered characteristic of a person or thing. It is also an appellation or descriptive term which is common in historical titles such as "Catherine the Great."

The term is taken from the Greek *epitheton,* meaning "attributed" or "added," and was formed by combining *epi,* meaning "on," and *tithenai,* meaning "to place."

Homer used many epithets, among them:

> "rosy-fingered dawn"
> "swift-footed Achilles"
> "all-seeing Jove."

Essay - a short literary composition on a particular theme or topic, usually in prose and generally thoughtful and interpretative. This

From Shakespeare's *A Midsummer Night's Dream*

type of writing is devoted to the presentation of the writer's own ideas and generally addresses a particular aspect of the subject.

The word is directly from the Latin *exagium*, meaning "weighing" or "trial by weight."

The essay is considered an invention of the European Renaissance, a product of the period's emphasis on the individual and the exploration of one's inner self in relation to the outside world. The term was first used by Montaigne in 1580 for informal reflections on himself and mankind in general called *Essaia*, which means "trying out" in French. Francis Bacon's *Essays* in 1597 were written as "counsels for the successful conduct of life and the management of men." Since the Seventeenth Century, English writers, such as Addison, Goldsmith, Lamb, Hazlitt, Steele, Chesterton, Huxley, and Orwell, have written essays.

Euphemism - the use of an indirect, mild, delicate, inoffensive, or vague word or expression for one thought to be coarse, sordid, or otherwise unpleasant, offensive, or blunt.

The word is from the Greek *euphemismos* derived from *euphemizein*, meaning "to speak words of good omen."

Common examples of euphemisms are "passed away" for died, "little girl/boy's room" for bathroom, and "terminal illness" for deadly illness.

Exegesis - a critical interpretation and explanation of a literary work, but usually applied to an analysis of an unusually difficult passage in poetry or prose. Exegesis refers especially to the interpretation and explanation of a selection from the Bible.

The word comes directly from the Greek and evolved from *exegeesthai*, meaning "to explain." That term was formed by combining *ex*, meaning" out," and *hegeesthai*, meaning "to guide."

In Roman times, exegetes were professional and official interpreters of charms, omens, dreams, sacred law, and oracular pronouncements.

Exposition - a form of discourse that explains, defines, and interprets. The word is also applied to the beginning portion of a plot in which background information about the characters and situation is set forth.

The word is taken directly from the Latin *exposition,* meaning "a showing forth."

Shakespeare's *Othello, Romeo and Juliet, Henry V,* and *Richard III* all contain exposition. Magazine articles, editorials, and essays usually consist almost wholly of exposition.

Fable - a short, simple story, usually with animals as characters, designed to teach a moral truth. Such a story often concludes with an epigram containing the moral. Allegories, parables, and fables with animals as the principal characters are sometimes called beast fables. Occasionally, the term is applied to stories about supernatural persons, to accounts of extraordinary events, to legends and myths, and to outright falsehoods.

The word is from the Latin *fabula* which was derived from *fari,* meaning "to speak."

The first collection of fables is ascribed to Aesop, who is said to have been a slave in the Sixth Century B.C. in Greece.

George Orwell's political satire *Animal Farm* (1945) is a fable.

see: *allegory, folklore, parable, proverb*

Fantasy - extravagant and unrestrained imagination. In writing, it is used to denote a literary work in which the action occurs in a nonexistent and unreal world (such as fairyland) or to a selection that involves incredible characters.

The word is from the Greek *phantasia,* meaning "making visible" which was derived from *phainein,* meaning "to show."

Science fiction and utopian stories are forms of fantasy. Fantasy writers include Lewis Carroll, Ray Bradbury, and H. P. Lovecraft.

see: *fable, science fiction*

Farce - a foolish show or a ridiculous sham. Also, a light, humorous play in which the plot depends upon a carefully exploited situation rather than upon character development. Farce is usually considered to be a boisterous comedy involving ludicrous action and dialogue which is intended to excite laughter through exaggeration and extravagance rather than by a realistic imitation of life. It contains exaggerated physical action which is often repeated, exaggeration of character and situation, absurd situations, and surprises in the form of unexpected appearances and disclosures. The characters and dialogue are almost always subservient to the plot and situation which are so complex that the events happen with bewildering rapidity. Elements of farce can be found in Classical Literature, and it is the mainstay of many television and film comedians.

The word comes from the Vulgar Latin *farsa* which was derived from *farcire*, meaning "to stuff viands (food)."

Farce was originally an impromptu interlude "stuffed in" between the parts of a more serious play and has been extant since Aristophanes. In Fifteenth Century France, farce was used by lay companies such as notaries and law clerks for their annual festivals.

Farce can be found in "The Miller's Tale" from Chaucer's *The Canterbury Tales*. Shakespeare also used farce in his *The Taming of the Shrew*. In this play, a wild, unhappy, angry, and seemingly incorrigible young woman is not only "tamed," but becomes a willing role model of womanhood and the young wife simply because her new husband has coerced her into this role; even in Shakespeare's time, this was considered a ridiculous supposition.

see: *the absurd, black comedy*

Fiction - any imagined and invented literary composition fashioned to entertain and possibly instruct. While fiction makes its readers think, its primary purpose is to make its readers feel. The most common elements of fiction are: point of view, characters, conflict, plot, and setting. The term is usually applied to novels and short stories, but drama, epic, fable, fairy tale, folklore, verse, and parable also contain fictional elements.

From Orwell's *Animal Farm*

The word is from the Latin *fictionem* which was derived from *fingere*, meaning "to shape" or "fashion."

Since fiction is imaginary, any novel, such as those of Austen, Brontë, Cather, or Conrad, may be included in this genre, in addition to any other "made-up" work of literature.

see: *allegory, ballad, comedy, drama, epic, fable, fairy tale, fantasy, folk tale, novel, parable, saga, science fiction, short story, story, tragedy*

Figure of speech (also called trope) - the expressive use of language in which words are used in other ways than their literal senses so as to suggest and produce pictures or images in a reader or hearer's mind, bypassing logic and appealing directly to the imagination in order to give particular emphasis to an idea or sentiment. There are three classes:

1. imagined similarities such as allegory, allusion, conceit, and simile
2. suggestive associations in which one work is linked with another such as hypallage, hyperbole, metonymy, and synecdoche
3. appeals to the ear and eye such as alliteration, anacoluthon, and onomatopoeia

Figures of speech may also be grouped into figures of thought in which words retain their meaning but not their rhetorical patterns.

Examples are given under each of the following listings.

see: *analogy, allegory, alliteration, allusion, conceit, irony, metaphor, onomatopoeia, simile*

First-person narrative - personal point of view of the first person, usually the author participant if the writer assumes the point of view of a character. The narrator is the "I" telling his/her part in the story such as in Charlotte Brontë's *Jane Eyre* (1847).

First is from the Middle English, from the Old English *fryst* which derived from *faran*, meaning "to go." Person has the same etymology as persona and is discussed there, while the etymology of narrative is discussed under that word.

see: *narrative, point of view*

Folklore - the long-standing and traditional beliefs, legends, and customs of a people. It is a general term for the verbal, spiritual, and material aspects of any culture that are transmitted orally, by observation, or by imitation, and passed on and preserved from generation to generation with constant variations shaped by memory, immediate need or purpose, and the degree of individual talent. Not only does folklore entertain, but it passes on the culture and behavior models of a people, which psychologist Carl Jung called "the collective unconscious." Folklore is comprised of folk tales.

The term comes from Old English *folc* which became Middle English *folk*, meaning "people," and the Anglo-Saxon *lar*, meaning "learning."

The word was coined in 1846 by the Englishman William John Thoms in *Athenaeum* to replace the word then being used: antiquities. Once this embraced only orally transmitted materials, but now includes written accounts of traditions, literature, craftsmanship, and folk habits. There is much folklore in ballads, epics, fables, fairy tales, maxima, myths, and riddles.

Shelley's *Frankenstein, Sir Gawain and the Green Knight,* Bram Stoker's *Dracula,* and Toni Morrison's *Beloved* are all heavily invested with elements of folklore.

see: *ballad, fairy tale, myth, proverb, riddle*

Folk tale - a traditional legend or narrative originating among a people, usually part of an oral tradition and subject to variation in transmission. Folk tales include legends, myths, fables, and the supernatural. Folk tales make up the folklore of a people.

The etymology of this word is the same as that of folklore.

Examples of folklore include the "Johnny Appleseed" and "Babe, the Blue Ox," stories of the Old West American culture.

see: *fable, folklore, legend, myth*

Formula - a fixed and conventional method of developing a plot. In films, television, and western stories, there are several stock formulas, including the redemption theme, the Cinderella story, and the country bumpkin plot. While formulas are hackneyed, stereotypical, and use the same conventions repeatedly, there are also formulas in the form of poems in the oral tradition. They are predictable and conform to the patterns of the genre.

Formula is Latin, a diminutive of *forma*, meaning "form."

An example of a formula plot is the traditional rags to riches story, such as found in the novel *Moll Flanders*.

Free verse - verse that lacks regular meter and line length but relies upon natural rhythms. It is free from fixed metrical patterns, but does reveal the cadences that result from alternating stressed and unstressed syllables. The form is thought to add force to thought and expression. While giving an address on May 17, 1935, Robert Frost explained, "Writing free verse is like playing tennis with the net down."

Free came through Middle English from the Old English *freo*, meaning "free." The etymology of verse is discussed under that listing.

Milton was experimenting with free verse in *Samson Agonistes*, and Walt Whitman used it in his "After the Sea-ship":

After the sea-ship, after the whistling winds,
After the white-grey sails taut to their spars and ropes,
Below, a myriad myriad waves hastening, lifting up their necks,
Tending in ceaseless flow toward the track of the ship,

From Shelley's *Frankenstein*

Waves of the ocean bubbling and gurgling, blithely prying,
Waves, undulating waves, liquid, uneven, emulous waves,
Toward that whirling current, laughing and buoyant, with
curves,
Where the great vessel sailing and tacking displace the
surface . . .

                                                        lines 1 – 8

Genre - a category or class of artistic endeavor having a particular
    form, technique, style, or content. Some current genres are the
    novel, short story, essay, epic, tragedy, comedy, satire, and lyric.

    The word is the French synonym for type and kind.

    Before the Eighteenth Century, the distinction between genres
was great. The accepted genres were epic, tragedy, lyric, comedy,
and satire. Today, there is less of a distinction between genres and
sometimes a work can contain elements of two or more genres.

    Wuthering Heights, by Emily Brontë, is considered to be part
of the gothic genre established at the end of the Nineteenth Century.

see: *comedy, epic, essay, novel, short story, tragedy*

Hagiography - a subtype of biography dealing with the lives and
    legends of saints and the critical study of these lives and leg-
    ends. There are two main groups: literary, such as *The Golden
    Legend of Jacobus a Voragine* of the Thirteenth Century, and
    liturgical, such as *The Roman Martyrology* of the late Sixteenth
    Century. A second definition for hagiography is any idealizing
    or worshipful biography.

    The word was formed by combining the Greek *hagio*, mean-
ing "saint or sacred," and *grapha*, meaning "written or writing
about."

Haiku (called hokku until the Nineteenth Century) - Japanese verse
    usually employing allusions and comparisons. The verse is

composed of three lines containing a fixed number of syllables, usually 17 or 19, within three unrhymed lines: five, seven, and five syllables per each line in order. The haiku presents a pair of contrasting images, one suggestive of time and place, the other a vivid but fleeting observation which, together, evoke mood and emotion.

The following example is from Bashō (pseudonym of Matsuo Munefusa 1644–94):

> Now the swinging bridge
> Is quieted with creepers . . .
> Like our tendrilled life.

The word evolved from *renga,* used extensively by Zen Buddhist monks in the Fifteenth and Sixteenth Centuries.

Hero - the principal character of a play, novel, etc.

In classical Greek, Hero was the priestess of Aphrodite, goddess of love, at Sestos, a town on the Hellespont—now the Dardanelles. She was loved by Leander, who lived at Abydos on the Asian side of the channel. Since they couldn't marry because of Hero's vow of chastity, Leander swam over to Europe nightly guided by the lamp in Hero's tower. One stormy night, the high winds blew out the light and he drowned. His body washed ashore beneath her tower, and she threw herself into the sea. In mythology, a hero is a man of godlike prowess and goodness who came to be honored as a divinity. Later, the word came to mean a warrior-chieftain of special strength, ability, and courage. Later still, hero meant an immortal being, or a demigod. During the last few centuries, the term evolved to mean a man of physical or moral courage, admired for bravery and noble deeds. Finally, the meaning evolved to the current definition offered above.

see: *antagonist, protagonist*

Homily - a moralizing discourse or sermon explaining some part of the Bible with accompanying instruction for the congregation.

The term is derived from the Greek *homilia*, meaning "converse or discourse."

Books of Homilies were published in 1547 and, again, in 1563 to be read in parish churches. Shakespeare refers to homilies in *As You Like It* when Rosalind comments on the verses Celia is reading :

> O most gentle pulpiter! What tedious homily of
> love have you wearied your parishioners withal,
> and never cried "Have patience, good people"!
>
> Act III, scene ii : lines 154 – 156

Hubris - arrogance, excessive self-pride and self-confidence. The word was used to refer to the emotions in Greek tragic heroes that led them to ignore warnings from the gods and thus invite catastrophe. It is considered a form of hamartia or tragic flaw that stems from overbearing pride and lack of piety.

The word is taken directly from the Greek *hubris*, meaning "insolence or pride."

The concept was used by Sophocles in his *The Oedipus Trilogy.* In this cycle of plays, Apollo, the God of Truth, warns King Laius of Thebes that he will be killed by his child. When Oedipus is born, his father exiles him but the child returns as an adult and kills Laius, not recognizing him as his father. King Laius invited catastrophe by attempting to circumvent Apollo's prophecy. The King's actions revealed his hubris because he, a mortal, thought he knew more than Apollo, a god.

Hyperbole - obvious and deliberate exaggeration or an extravagant statement. It is a figure of speech not intended to be taken literally since it is exaggeration for the sake of emphasis. Hyperbole is a common poetic and dramatic device.

The word is from the Greek *huperbole*, meaning "overshooting" which was derived from *huperballein*, meaning "to throw beyond" or "to exceed."

From Brontë's *Wuthering Heights*

The device was common in Tudor and Jacobean drama and is an essential part of burlesque. Shakespeare used it in *Antony and Cleopatra* when Cleopatra praises the dead Antony:

> His legs bestrid the ocean; his reared arm
> Crested the world . . . .
>
> Act V, scene ii : lines 82 – 83

Hyperbole is consistently used in everyday speech, such as when saying, "I'm freezing." when you are cold.

see: *bombast, irony*

Idiom - the language, dialect, or style of speaking peculiar to a people or the constructions or expressions of one language whose structure is not matched in another language. Idioms often possess a meaning other than their grammatical or logical ones and cannot be directly translated into another language. It also is used to describe something peculiar to an individual.

The word comes from the Greek *idioma*, meaning "a peculiarity in language" which was derived from *idio*, and *omai*, together meaning "make one's own."

In the original Greek, the word was used to mean either a private citizen or something belonging to a private citizen, hence, personal.

Some examples in English are "no wonder," "better late than never," "to lead by the nose," and "spick and span."

see: *colloquialism*

Imagery - the forming of mental images, figures, or likenesses of things. It is also the use of language to represent actions, persons, objects, and ideas descriptively. This means encompassing the senses also, rather than just forming a mental picture.

The word is from the Latin *imago*, meaning "to image," and *imitari*, meaning "to imitate."

Examples of imagery may be found under the listings below.

see: *archetype, connotation, metaphor, simile*

In medias res - beginning a narrative well along in the sequence of events. It is a convention used in epic poetry and sometimes novels, short stories, drama, and narrative poetry designed to attract immediate attention from and secure the prompt interest of the reader or audience.

The phrase is Latin and means "in the middle of things."

The Iliad begins in the final year of the Trojan War, with Homer recounting the beginning of the war later in the epic. Milton used *in medias res* in *Paradise Lost* by beginning his narrative in Hell after the rebel angels have fallen.

Interior monologue - represents the inner thoughts of a character, recording the internal or emotional thoughts or feelings of an individual.

Interior is from the Old Latin *interus*, meaning "inward" or "on the inside." The etymology of monologue is discussed under the listing for that term.

William Faulkner uses interior monologue in his novels, such as *The Sound and the Fury*, and even comments on the impressions passing through the minds of his characters.

see: *monologue*

Irony - a dryly humorous or lightly sarcastic figure of speech in which the literal meaning of a word or statement is the opposite of that intended. In literature, it is the technique of indicating an intention or attitude opposed to what is actually stated. Often, only the context of the statement leads the reader to understand it is ironic. Irony makes use of hyperbole, sarcasm, satire, and understatement. There are four types of irony:

1. verbal irony as defined by Cicero (see below)
2. situational irony, such as when a pickpocket gets his own pockets picked
3. dramatic irony, such as when Oedipus unwittingly kills his own father
4. rhetorical irony, such as that of the innocent narrator in Twain's *Huckleberry Finn*

The term is taken directly from the Greek *eironeia*, meaning "simulated ignorance."

The term was first recorded in *Plato's Republic* in the Fourth Century B.C. Aristotle described it as "a dissembling toward the inner core of truth" while Cicero defined it by saying, "Irony is the saying of one thing and meaning another." Socratic irony is when one adopts another's point of view in order to reveal that person's weaknesses and eventually to ridicule him.

Alexander Pope made use of irony when writing in the Eighteenth Century periodical *The Guardian*. Under a false name, Pope wrote an ironic review of rival poet Ambrose Phillips, juxtaposing Phillip's worst work with his own best verse - all the while effusively maintaining the superiority of Phillips.

see: *hyperbole, satire*

Lampoon - prose or verse, sometimes in the form of sharp satire, which severely ridicules the character, intentions, or behavior of a person, institution, or society. Lampoons appeared often in the Seventeenth and Eighteenth Centuries, but are less common today because of libel laws.

The term is taken from the Old French *lampon* which was derived from *lampos*, meaning "let us guzzle (used as a refrain in derogatory songs)."

Dryden lampoons Shadwell, whom he names Og in "Absalom and Achitophel - Part II."

> Now stop your noses, Readers, all and some,
> For here's a tun of Midnight work to come,

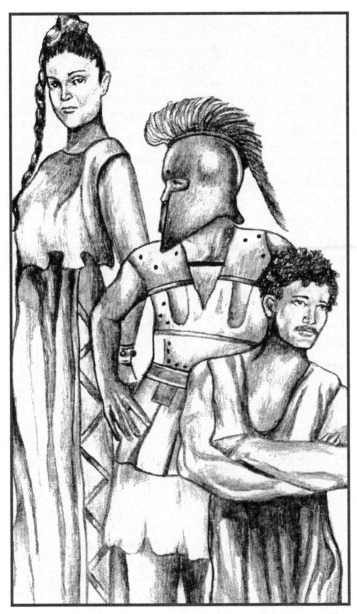

From *Plato's Republic*

Og from a Treason Tavern rowling home.
Round as a Globe and Liquored ev'ry chink,
Goodly and Great he Sayls behind his Link,
With all this Bulk there's nothing lost in Og,
For ev'ry inch that is not Fool is Rogue:
A Monstrous mass of foul corrupted matter,
As all the Devils had spew'd to make the batter,
When wine has given him courage to Blaspheme,
He curses God, but God before curst him;
And if man cou'd have reason, none has more,
That made his Paunch so rich and him so poor.

lines 457 – 469

Legend - a tradition or story handed down from earlier times and popularly accepted as true but actually a mix of fact and fiction. The term is also applied to any fictitious tale concerning a real person, event, or place and is likely to be less concerned with the supernatural than a myth. Another definition of legend is brief, explanatory comments accompanying a photograph, map, or painting; in such a case, a synonym is caption.

The term comes from the Medieval Latin *legenda*, meaning "to be read," which was derived from *legere*, meaning "to read."

Originally, the term denoted a story about a saint which was read aloud during the services of the early Christian church.

Among the many Greek legends are the epics of Homer: *The Iliad* and *The Odyssey*. Some legendary characters are King Arthur and the Knights of the Round Table, Robin Hood, and Beowulf.

see: *folklore, hagiography, myth*

Limerick - light verse consisting of a stanza of five lines, rhyming aabba, which is usually naughty in nature. The first, second, and fifth lines are in trimeter, and the third and fourth lines are in dimeter. Limericks are almost always humorous in tone.

The term takes its name from a county in Ireland and social gatherings there, at which nonsense verse was set out in facetious jingles.

Limericks first appeared in print in *Anecdotes and Adventures of Fifteen Young Ladies* and *The History of Sixteen Wonderful Old Women* in 1820. They were popularized by Edward Lear in two of his books: *Book of Nonsense* and *More Nonsense.*

An example is the following by Langford Reed:

> An indolent vicar of Bray
> His roses allowed to decay.
> His wife, more alert,
> Bought a powerful squirt
> And said to her spouse, "Let us spray."

Litany - a form of prayer consisting of a series of invocations with identical responses in succession. It is also the term for the supplications in *The Book of Common Prayer* of the Church of England. Often, it is used for a recitation that is ceremonial and repetitive. It is common to hear the term used to describe any repetitive, monotonous statement or account.

The term comes from the Greek *litaneia* derived from *litaneuein,* meaning "to pray."

The form originated at Antioch in the Fourth Century.

Literal - pertaining to a letter of the alphabet. More typically, it means "based on what is actually written or expressed." A literal interpretation gives an exact rendering—word for word—taking words in their usual or primary sense. It is also used to describe thinking which is unimaginative or matter of fact.

The term is taken from the Latin *litteralis* derived from *littera,* meaning "letter of the alphabet."

Literature - writings in which expression and form, in connection with ideas and concerns of universal and apparently permanent interest, are essential features. While applied to any kind of printed material, such as circulars, leaflets, and handbills, there are some who feel it is more correctly reserved for prose and verse of acknowledged excellence, such as George Eliot's works. The term connotes superior qualities.

The etymology of *literature* is the same as that of *literal* and may be found under that listing.

Any novel, such as Hardy's *Jude the Obscure* or *Tess of the D'Urbervilles,* may be considered literature.

Malapropism - the act or habit of misusing words to comic effect. This usually results from ignorance or from confusion of words similar in sound but different in meaning, mainly polysyllabic words.

The term is taken directly from the French *mal a propos*, meaning "inappropriate."

Mrs. Malaprop is a character in Sheridan's play *The Rivals* (1775) who chronically makes such mistakes. Dogberry the Watch in Shakespeare's *Much Ado About Nothing* (c. 1598) says "Comparisons are odorous," and later, "It shall be siffigance"—both malapropisms.

Melodrama - a form of play that intensifies sentiment, exaggerates emotions, and relates sensational and thrilling action with four basic sharply contrasted and simplified characters: the hero, the heroine, their comic ally, and a villain. The action is constantly kept at high tension.

The term is from the French *melodrame* which was derived from the Greek *melos*, meaning "song."

Originally, melodramas were Roman plays with music, song, and dance. In the Eighteenth Century, the form evolved into productions with elaborate but oversimplified and coincidental romantic plots without regard for character development or logic, but having much sentimentality and sometimes a happy ending. The first in England was the 1802 *A Tale of Mystery.* Harriet Beecher Stowe's *Uncle Tom's Cabin*, written in 1853, is also considered a melodrama.

Metaphor - a figure of speech in which a word or phrase is applied to a person, idea, or object to which it is not literally applicable. It is an implied analogy or unstated comparison which imaginatively identifies one thing with another. This device is used by an author to turn or twist the meaning of a word. Metaphors are the most often used figure of speech. While not required in poetry, they are universally used there. A "dead metaphor" is a former metaphor now accepted as common usage, such as table leg or car hood.

The term is from the Greek *metaphora*, meaning "transference" which was formed by combining *meta*, meaning "over" and *pherein*, meaning "to carry."

John Donne makes use of metaphor when he writes in *Twickenham Garden*:

> And take my tears, which are love's wine.
>
> line 20

see: *analogy, connotation, metaphor, simile*

Monologue - refers to a speech by one person in a drama, a form of entertainment by a single speaker, or an extended part of the text of a play uttered by an actor.

The term is taken directly from the Greek *monologos*, meaning "speaking alone."

An example is Macbeth's questioning of his own sanity in Shakespeare's *Macbeth*:

> Is this a dagger which I see before me,
> The handle toward my hand? Come, let me clutch thee!
> I have thee not, and yet I see thee still.
> Art thou not, fatal vision, sensible
> To feeling as to sight? or art thou but
> A dagger of the mind, a false creation,
> Proceeding from the heat-oppressed brain?
>
> Act II, scene i : lines 42 – 48

see: *dialogue, interior monologue, soliloquy*

Morality play - an allegory in dramatic form. Popular from the Fourteenth to the Sixteenth Centuries, most morality plays used personified abstractions of vices and virtues. They did not necessarily use the Bible or strictly religious material and were more concerned with morality than spirit. This type of play essentially depicted a battle between the forces of good and evil in the human soul.

The word "morality" comes from the Latin *moralis* which was derived from *mor* or *mos*, meaning "custom." The word play comes from the Old English *plegan*, meaning "to play."

The morality play had its dramatic origins in the Mystery and Miracle plays of the late Middle Ages. Its allegorical origins were from sermon literature and other works of spiritual education.

Everyman (c. 1510) is the most common, but was preceded by *Castle of Perseverance* (c. 1420). The legacy of the morality play may be seen in Shakespeare's Iago, from *Othello,* who resembles the Vice in morality plays.

see: *allegory*

Muse - the genius or powers characteristic of a literary artist, or a goddess regarded as inspiring a poet or other writer. In classical mythology, the Muses were the nine daughters of Zeus and Mnemosyne (the Goddess of Memory) who presided over them. Each daughter was considered the inspiration in a different area: Calliope—epic poetry; Euterpe—lyric poetry; Clio—history; Terpsichore—choral songs and the dance; Melpomene—tragedy; Erato—love poetry; Polyhymnia—sacred poetry; Thalia—comedy; and Urania—astronomy. They were said to be the companions of the Graces and Apollo, the god of music.

The term is from the Greek *mousa*, meaning "men" which was derived from *mon*, meaning "think" or "remember."

Homer's *Iliad* opens with an appeal to a muse, and John Milton, in his *Paradise Lost*, also appeals to one of the muses:

> Descend from Heav'n Urania, by that name
> If rightly thou art call'd, whose Voice divine

Following, above th' Olympian Hill I soare,
Above the flight of Pegasean wing.

Book 7 : lines 1 – 4

Another example is in Shakespeare's prologue to *Henry V*:

O for a Muse of fire that would ascend
The brightest heaven of invention!

Act I, scene i : lines 1 – 2

Myth - a legendary or traditional story, usually one concerning a superhuman being and dealing with events that have no natural explanation. A myth may also be an unproved belief that is accepted uncritically, or an invented idea or story. It usually attempts to explain a phenomenon or strange occurrence without regard to fact or common sense and appeals to the emotions rather than reason. A myth is less historical than a legend and usually persists through oral transmission, as do legends and fables.

The term is taken directly from the Greek *muthos,* meaning "fable."

Moby-Dick by Herman Melville may be considered a myth. The Greek myth of Apollo driving his chariot across the sky is an early attempt to explain the rising and setting of the sun. Another Greek myth—that of Zeus throwing his thunderbolts—is an attempt to explain lightning and thunder.

see: *legend*

Narrative - a form of discourse which relates an event or series of events. Narratives need a narrator to communicate with the reader or hearer. The term is usually applied to anecdotes, exemplums, fables, fabliaux, fairy tales, incidents, legends, novels, novelettes, short stories, and tales. The primary and basic appeal of narration is to the emotions of the reader or hearer.

The term is from the Latin *gnarus,* which means "knowing."

A novel/autobiography such as Angelou's *I Know Why the Caged Bird Sings* is considered a narrative.

see: *fiction, plot*

Nemesis (sometimes called fate) - in classical mythology, Nemesis was the Goddess of Divine Retributive Justice or Vengeance. Written with a small letter, the term means a rival or opponent who cannot be overcome. It also means any situation or condition that one cannot change or triumph over and an agent or act of punishment.

The term is from the Greek *nemesis,* meaning "retribution" and *nemein,* meaning "to deal out" or "dispense."

In Shakespeare's *Macbeth,* Macduff is the nemesis of Macbeth and Lady Macbeth.

see: *tragedy*

Noh (also spelled No) - the classic drama of Japan, comprised of one or two acts, either prose or verse, with a chorus contributing poetical comments, which was formerly acted only at the Shogun's court. Five or six were acted in succession, presenting a complete life drama: a divine age representation, a battle piece, a women's play, a psychological piece, a morality play, and a congratulatory piece praising the lords and the reign. Each was designed to evoke a certain mood and used symbolic gestures and chanting. There are about 200 Noh plays extant, traditionally written by Kwanami and his son, Seami. There were no female Noh actors; males played the female roles. The actors wore masks. This form of drama was recently revived. It is comparable with early Greek drama in that it is formal, restrained, subtle, symbolical, and spiritual.

The term is directly from the Japanese *noh,* meaning "skill" or "accomplishment."

Noh developed in the Fourteenth Century from ritual dances associated with ancient Shinto worship. The form was perfected in the Fifteenth Century.

Nom de plume (also called pseudonym) - the assumed name under which an author writes.

From Melville's *Moby-Dick*

The term is taken from the French *nom de plume*, meaning "pen name" but does not actually exist in the French language— which uses *nom de guerre*, meaning "assumed name under which a person fights or writes."

Several well-known *nom de plumes* are Mark Twain (Samuel L. Clemens); George Orwell (Eric Blair); and George Eliot (Mary Ann Evans).

Novel - a lengthy fictitious prose narrative portraying characters and presenting an organized series of events and settings. Novels are accounts of life and involve conflict, characters, action, settings, plot, and theme. This is considered the third stage of the development of imagination fiction, following the epic and the romance.

The term is from the Latin *novellus* which is a diminutive of *novus*, meaning "new."

The term was used during the early Renaissance for any new story. The first great novel of the Western world was that of Spain's Miguel de Cervantes: *Don Quixote de la Mancha,* written from 1605 to 1612. Early novels were often heavily moralistic, intended to teach the reader a lesson about human nature.

Daniel Defoe wrote the novels *Robinson Crusoe* and *Moll Flanders* in Eighteenth-Century England, but the form was firmly established in England later in the same century with Samuel Richardson's *Pamela* (1740). In the Nineteenth Century, Dickens serialized his novels, making them overwhelmingly popular.

Ode - a lyric poem with a dignified theme that is phrased in a for- mal, elevated style. Its purpose is to praise and glorify. Odes describe nature intellectually rather than emotionally and usually consist of a succession of stanzas in lines of varying length and meter.

The term comes from the Greek *oide* or *aoide,* which was de- rived from *aeidein,* meaning "to sing."

Originally, an ode was a poem meant to be sung. The earliest ode-like poems were written by Sappho c. 600 B.C. and Alcaeus c. 611 – 580 B.C., while the modern ode dates from the Renaissance. Interest in this poetry form revived in the Twentieth Century.

John Milton's "On the Morning of Christ's Nativity" is an ode.

Onomatopoeia - the formation and use of words that suggest, by their sounds, the object or idea being named or the imitation of natural sounds by words such as "bang" or "buzz." It is a figure of speech and is especially useful for rhetorical effect.

The term is from the Greek *onomatopoiia* which was formed by joining *onoma*, meaning "name," and *poiein*, meaning "to make."

Words such as whinny, splash, and knock are examples of onomatopoeia. Dylan Thomas uses this technique in his "Fern Hill" (emphasis added):

> Out of the <u>whinnying</u> green stable
> On to the fields of praise.
>
> lines 35 – 36

Oral tradition (also called oral transmission) - the spreading or passing on of material by word of mouth. Original works were once made known to audiences only by recitation, singing, and memory rather than in the written form. Many folk tales, fables, proverbs, and songs were first the property of common people who repeated or sang them, altering them by accident or on purpose, and taught them to the next generation, and so on. Oral tradition is usually the product of an illiterate or semi-literate society. This is the earliest of all forms of poetry since it preceded written poetry and is still alive in many parts of the world.

The term is made up of two words: oral from the Latin *or* or *os*, meaning "mouth," and *tradition* from the Latin *traditio*, meaning "action of handing over."

From Defoe's *Moll Flanders*

An interesting fictional example of oral tradition can be found at the end of Ray Bradbury's *Fahrenheit 451*. Examples of works of oral tradition may also be found under the listings below.

see: *ballad, epic, figure of speech, folklore, formula*

Oratory - the rendering of a formal speech delivered on a special occasion, characterized by elevated style and diction and by studied delivery. Sometimes the term simply means an eloquent address.

The term is from the Latin *orare*, meaning "to pray."

An example of oratory is found in Shakespeare's *Julius Caesar*, when Mark Antony speaks to his countrymen about his slain friend:

> Friends, Romans, countrymen, lend me your ears
> I come to bury Caesar, not to praise him.
> The evil that men do lives after them;
> The good is oft interred with their bones;
> So let it be with Caesar . . .
>
> Act III, scene ii : lines 75 – 79

Oxymoron - a figure of speech in which two contradictory words or phrases are combined to produce a rhetorical effect by means of a concise paradox.

The term comes from the Greek *oxumoros*, meaning pointedly foolish which was formed by combining *oxus*, meaning sharp, and *moros*, meaning foolish.

An example is the word *sophomore* which is a combination of two Greek words: *sophos*, which means "wise," and *moros*, which means "foolish." In Shakespeare's Sonnet 142, the speaker declares:

> "Love is my sin, and thy dear virtue hate."
>
> Line 1

see: *antithesis, paradox*

Palindrome - a word, sentence, or verse reading the same backward as forward—excluding punctuation.

The term is from the Greek *palindromos*, meaning "running back again" which was formed by combining *palin*, meaning "again," and *drom*, meaning "run." The most common examples are the word "civic" and the phrase "Madam, I'm Adam." The best known collection of palindromes was produced by Ambrose Pamperis in 1802; it contains 416 palindrome verses telling about the campaigns of Catherine the Great.

Parable - a short, simple story designed to convey some religious principle, moral lesson, or general truth by comparison with actual events. A parable is often an allegory in which each character represents an abstract concept—such as obedience or honesty—and is illustrated through real-life events.

The term is from the Greek *parabole*, meaning "comparison" or "putting beside" which was derived from *paraballein*, meaning "to throw beside."

Melville's *Billy Budd* is sometimes offered as a parable since it demonstrates that absolute good may not co-exist with absolute evil. In this novel, Billy is an innocent, impressionable, young sailor, the personification of absolute good. He is court-martialed and hanged for mutiny and murder under trumped-up charges brought against him by Claggart, the personification of absolute evil.

see: *allegory, fable*

Paradox - a statement that is apparently self-contradictory or absurd but really contains a possible truth. Sometimes the term is applied to a self-contradictory false proposition. It is also used to describe an opinion or statement which is contrary to generally accepted ideas. Often, a paradox is used to make a reader consider the point in a new way.

The term is from the Greek *paradoxos*, meaning "contrary to received opinion" or "expectation."

An example of paradox is contained in Caesar's speech from Shakespeare's *Julius Caesar:*

> Cowards die many times before their deaths.
>
> Act II, scene ii : line 32

see: *epigram, oxymoron*

Parallelism - an arrangement of the parts of a composition so that elements of equal importance are balanced in similar constructions. This arrangement may be applied to words, phrases, clauses, sentences, paragraphs, or complete units of compositions. Parallelism is a rhetorical device.

The term comes from the Greek *parallelos*, meaning "beside one another."

Shakespeare used this device in his *Richard II* when King Richard laments his position:

> I'll give my jewels for a set of beads,
> My gorgeous palace for a hermitage,
> My gay apparel for an almsman's gown,
> My figured goblets for a dish of wood . . . .
>
> Act III, scene iii : lines 170 – 173

see: *antithesis, subplot*

Paraphrase (also called rewording) - the restatement of a passage giving the meaning in another form. This usually involves expanding the original text so as to make it clear.

The term is from the Greek *paraphrasis*, meaning literally, "beside phrase," and "beside speech."

In contemporary usage, paraphrase normally is synonymous with rewarding.

Parody - a humorous, satirical, or burlesque imitation of a person, event, or serious work of literature designed to ridicule in non-sensical fashion or to criticize by clever duplication. The term is also used for a comic imitation of a serious poem, similar to cartoon caricature of a person's face.

The term is from the Greek *paroidia*, meaning "burlesque poem or song."

This technique has been traced back as far as ancient Greek. "The Nun's Priest's Tale" from Chaucer's *The Canterbury Tales*, as well as some of Swift's and Joyce's works, are parodies.

see: *lampoon*

Pastoral - an artistic composition dealing with the life of shepherds or with a simple, rural existence. It is also a work of art representing the idealized life of shepherds to create an image of a peaceful and uncorrupted existence. In addition, the term is used to describe simplicity, charm, and serenity attributed to country life. Currently, it applies to any literary convention that places kindly, rural people in nature-centered activities.

The term is from the Latin *pastor*, meaning "shepherd."

The rural settings and characters originate from folk songs and ceremonies that honored the pastoral gods. Theocritus (316 – 260 B.C.) first used the convention in his *Idylls*. *As You Like It*, written by Shakespeare in 1600, is also considered a pastoral.

Persona - a character in drama or fiction or the part any one sustains in the world or in a book. Persona also denotes the "I" who speaks in a poem or novel.

The term is from the Latin *persona*, meaning "actor's mask," "character acted," or "human being."

The term was used in Jungian psychology as "Public personality," which means the facade or mask presented to the world, but not representative of inner feelings and emotions. Two well-known

From Melville's *Billy Budd*

personas are the narrator in Chaucer's *Canterbury Tales* and Gulliver of Swift's *Gulliver's Travels*.

see: *monologue, point of view*

Personification - a figure of speech in which abstractions, animals, ideas, and inanimate objects are endowed with human form, character, traits, or sensibilities. An entirely imaginary creature or person also may be conceived of as representing an idea or object. Like a metaphor, personification is a frequent resource in poetry.

The etymology of this term is the same as that of persona.

A colloquial example of personification is when one refers to a car as "she." Another example of personification is "the wind shrieked through the window."

see: *allegory*

Plagiarism - literary theft, which is the taking or closely imitating of the language and thoughts of another author and representing them as one's own—even if this is done without conscious thought. This includes self-plagiarism, which is unwittingly borrowing from your own work. While common among Elizabethan dramatists, it is now prevented by copyright laws.

The term is directly from the Latin *plagiarius*, meaning "kidnapper."

Plot - a plan or scheme to accomplish a purpose. In literature, this is the arrangement of events to achieve an intended effect consisting of a series of carefully devised and interrelated actions that progresses through a struggle of opposing forces, called conflict, to a climax and a denouement. This is different from story or story line which is the order of events as they occur.

The term is taken from the French *complot*, meaning "conspiracy. "

Aristotle insisted plot must have a beginning, a middle, and an end, and that its events constitute a whole entity.

The plot of Miller's *The Crucible* involves a group of teenage girls who are discovered dancing naked in the woods by the town minister. Knowing that the punishment for their behavior will be severe, the girls claim that they were possessed by the spirits of members of the community who are trying to initiate them into witchcraft. Because of the gravity of the accusations (witchcraft is punishable by hanging), a court is set up to determine the guilt or innocence of those accused.

Poetic justice - the ideal distribution of rewards and punishments.

The term is formed by combining two words. The first is "poetic," which is from the Latin *poeta*, which may be further traced to the Greek *poietes*, meaning "poet" or "maker." The second is "justice," which is from the Latin *justitis* which was derived from *justus*, meaning "right" or "law."

The concept was first used in the Seventeenth Century to express the notion that, in literature, good should be rewarded and evil punished. The term itself was first used by the critic Thomas Rhymer in *Tragedies of the Last Age Consider'd* (1678).

Dickens brings poetic justice into play in *Great Expectations* when Pip, who has spent much of the novel avoiding his vulgar origins and distancing himself, sometimes cruelly, from his humble past, discovers that his benefactor is an ex-convict, Magwitch.

Poetic license - a liberty taken by a writer to produce a desired effect by deviating from conventional form, established rule, fact, or logic.

The etymology of "poetic" is discussed above. "License" is from Middle English, where it arrived from the Middle French *licence* which was derived from the Latin *licentia*, meaning "to be permitted."

An example of poetic license is when a poet forces a rhyme in a couplet such as the anonymous:

> My father once had a dog
> Who fell while sitting on a log.

Other examples of poetic license are the poetic contractions "O'er" and "E'er."

Poetry - a literary work in metrical form or patterned language. The term is also used to describe the art of rhythmical composition, written or spoken, which is designed to produce pleasure through beautiful, elevated, imaginative, or profound thoughts.

The etymology of "poetry" is the same as that of "poetic" discussed under "poetic justice."

Aristotle divided poetry into three genres which have each spawned other genres:

1. epic, which included narratives of heroic action and events of more than personal significance
2. lyric, which was originally meant to be sung
3. satire, which was the moral censure of evil, pretension, or anti-social behavior

Shakespeare discusses poetry in his *A Midsummer Night's Dream* when Theseus speaks of love:

> The lunatic, the lover, and the poet
> Are of imagination all compact.
> One sees more devils than vast hell can hold;
> Sees Helen's beauty in a brow of Egypt.
> The poet's eye, in a fine frenzy rolling,
> Doth glance from heaven to earth, from earth to heaven;
> And as imagination bodies forth
> The forms of things unknown, the poet's pen
> Turns them to shapes and gives to airy nothing
> A local habitation and a name.
>
>   Act V, scene i : lines 7 – 17

Point of view - a specified position or method of consideration and appraisal. It may also be an attitude, judgment, or opinion. In literature, physical point of view has to do with the position in time and space from which a writer approaches, views, and describes his or her material. Mental point of view involves an author's feeling and attitude toward his or her subject. Personal point of view concerns the relation through which a writer narrates or discusses a subject, whether first, second, or third person. If personal point of view is used and the writer assumes the point of view of a character, the author is writing in the first person. If the author takes the point of view of an observing character, the author is writing in the second person. If an impersonal point of view is taken, the author detaches himself completely and is an omniscient author, or third person. Sometimes authors employ several points of view in the same work.

The term is a phrase containing several words. Point came through Middle English from the Old French *pointe*, meaning "sharp edge," which was derived from the Latin *pungere*, meaning "to prick." View is also from Middle English, but through the Middle French *voir* which was derived from the Latin *videre*, meaning "to see."

Toni Morrison's *Beloved* is written from the point of view of the protagonist, Sethe. Hemingway's *To Have and To Have Not* is written from multiple perspectives.

see: *first-person narrative*

Prologue - the opening section of a longer work. It also means the preface or introductory part of a novel, long poem, or play.

The term is from the Greek *prologos* formed by *pro*, meaning "before," and *logos*, meaning "speech."

In ancient Greek tragedy, the prologue was the part of a play that set forth the subject of the drama before the chorus entered. Prologues were common in the Seventeenth and Eighteenth Centuries, usually in verse—except for plays, when a chorus was used.

The most famous example of a prologue in English is Chaucer's "General Prologue" in *The Canterbury Tales*. In this, Chaucer provides a background and setting for what is to follow as well as detailed sketches of the characters.

see: *epilogue*

Prose - the ordinary form of spoken and written language whose unit is the sentence, rather than the line as it is in poetry. The term applies to all expressions in language that do not have a regular rhythmic pattern.

The term is from the Latin *prosa*, meaning "in phrase" which was derived from *prosa oratio*, meaning "straight, direct, unadorned speech," which itself was derived from *prorsus*, meaning "straightforward or direct" and can be further traced to *pro versusm*, meaning "turned forward."

Novels, essays, short stories, and works of criticism are examples of prose.

see: *comedy, drama, essay, fable, fiction, folk tale, hagiography, legend, literature, myth, narrative, novel, saga, science fiction, short story, story, theme, tragedy*

Protagonist - the leading character of a drama, novel, etc. This is not always the hero, but is always the principal and central character whose rival is the antagonist.

The term is from the Greek *protagonistes*, meaning "first actor in a drama."

The Greek tragic poet was restricted to three actors: protagonist, deuteragonist, and tritagonist, or first, second, and third actor. In contests between actors, only the protagonists were considered.

Originally, Greek drama probably consisted of only a Chorus and the leader of the Chorus. Thespis (Sixth Century B.C.) added the first actor, Aeschylus the second, and Sophocles the third.

Some famous protagonists are Hester Prynne from Hawthorne's *The Scarlet Letter*, Atticus Finch from Lee's *To Kill a Mockingbird*, and the title character of *Hamlet*.

see: *antagonist*

Proverb - a short saying, usually of unknown or ancient origin, that expresses some useful thought, commonplace truth, or moral lesson and is most often expressed in simple, homely language. Sometimes, it is allegorical or symbolic. A proverb is appealing because it is succinct and uses simple rhyme, irony, metaphor, and comparison or contrast. Proverbs are common to almost all nations and peoples.

The term is from the Latin *proverbium* derived from *verbum*, meaning "word."

Proverbs are rooted in folklore and preserved by oral tradition.

The best known collection is *The Book of Proverbs* following *The Psalms* in *The Old Testament*.

see: *aphorism, epigram*

Pun (also called paronomasia) - a play on words or the humorous use of a word emphasizing a different meaning or application. They have been called by some "the lowest form of humor."

The term comes from combining two Greek words: *para*, meaning "beside," and *onomasia*, meaning "naming."

Puns have appeared in literature since Homer's writings in the Eighth Century B.C.

There is a famous pun uttered by Mercutio as he is dying in Shakespeare's *Romeo and Juliet*:

"Ask for me tomorrow and you shall find me a grave man."
                                                    Act III, scene i : lines 97 – 98

Pyrrhic - a metrical foot of two short unaccented syllables which is common in classical poetry. Most often, it is used as an adjective, applying to a victory won at too great a cost. It also means an ancient Greek warlike dance in which the motions of combat were imitated, much like Native North American war-dances.

From Morrison's *Beloved*

The term is from the Greek *purrhikhios* derived from *purrhikhe* which is said to be named for Purrhikhos, the inventor of a war-dance of the ancient Greeks.

Pyrrhus, King of Epirus, won a notable battle over the Romans at Asculum in the Third Century B.C. but lost so many men that he allegedly said, "One more such victory and we are lost."

Realism - the theory of writing in which the familiar, ordinary aspects of life are depicted in a matter of fact, straightforward manner designed to reflect life as it actually is. Realism often presents a careful description of everyday life, often concerning itself with the lives of the so-called middle or lower classes. According to Henry James, the main tenet of realism is that writers must not select facts in accord with preconceived aesthetics or ethical ideals but, rather, record their observations impartially and objectively. Realism downplays plot in favor of character and to concentrate on middle-class life and pre-occupations. It became an important tradition in theater through the works of Ibsen and Shaw, among others. However, realism is most often associated with the novel.

The term is from the Latin *realis*, meaning "belonging to the thing itself."

The movement began in the mid-Nineteenth Century in reaction to the highly subjective approach of romanticism, which was produced in Europe and the United States from about 1840 until the 1890s. Mark Twain was one of the pioneers of realism in the United States; other prominent American realists include Henry James, Edith Wharton, and William Dean Howells.

Refrain - a phrase or verse recurring at intervals in a poem or song, usually at the end of a stanza, which may help to establish the meter of a poem, indicate its tone, or reestablish its atmosphere. It may also be a nonsense line such as that in Shakespeare's *As You Like It*: "With a hey, and a ho, and a hey nonino," or a word or phrase that takes on added significance each time it appears.

The term is from the Old French *refraindre*, meaning "to restrain," "check," or to "repeat." This word was derived from the Low Latin *refringere*, meaning "to break back".

The refrain is very old, appearing in *The Egyptian Book of the Dead* and the Bible.

Rhetoric - the theory and principles concerned with the effective use of language or the theory and practice of eloquence, both written and oral. It consists of the rules that govern all prose composition or speech designed to influence the judgment or feelings of people, but is only loosely connected with specific details of mechanics, grammar, etc.; it is concerned with a consideration of the fundamental principles according to which oratorical discourses are composed: invention, arrangement, style, memory, and delivery.

The term is from the Greek *rhetorike* or *rhetor*, meaning "an orator," especially a professional one.

The actual founder of rhetoric as a science is said to be Corax of Syracuse in 465 B.C., while Homer is considered the Father of Oratory. To the ancient Greeks, rhetoric was essential for argumentation and oratory. By the medieval era, it became one of the trivium of The Seven Liberal Arts (the other two were grammar and logic) taught at universities. According to Aristotelian theory, rhetoric was a way of organizing material for the presentation of the truth. Socrates, conversely, considered it a superficial art.

Rhetoric was used by Nestor, Odysseus, and, in Homer's *Iliad*, Achilles. Satan makes use of rhetoric in *Paradise Lost* when, in the form of a serpent, he attempts to persuade Eve that eating the forbidden fruit will not kill her:

> "ye shall not die: How should ye? By the fruit?
>   It gives you life
> To knowledge; by the threatener? look on mee,
> mee who have touch'd and tasted,
>   yet both lives.
> And life more perfect have attained than fate
> meant mee."

Book IX: lines 685-690

Rhetorical question - one asked solely to produce an effect or to make a statement, but not expected to receive an answer. The purpose to such a question, whose answer is obvious, is usually to make a deeper impression upon the hearer or reader than a direct statement would.

The etymology of rhetorical is the same as that of rhetoric, as discussed above. The second word of the term, "question," is from the Latin *quaestio* derived from *quarere*, meaning "to seek or ask."

In Shakespeare's *The Merchant of Venice*, Shylock uses rhetorical questions in his famous speech:

> Hath not
> a Jew eyes? hath not a Jew hands, organs,
> dimensions, senses, affections, passions? . . .
> If you prick us, do we not bleed? if you tickle us,
> do we not laugh? if you poison us, do we not die?
> And if you wrong us, shall we not revenge?
>
> Act III, scene i : lines 55 – 63

Rhyme - the similarity or identity of terminal sound in words. In the most common form, two words rhyme when their accented vowels and all succeeding sounds are identical. This provides pleasing sense impressions and serves as an element of rhythm emphasizing the beat. Rhyme is the commonest and most ancient form of metrical devices.

The term is from the Greek *rhuthmos* derived from the Latin *rhythmus*, meaning measured motion or rhythm.

In the Fourteenth Century, rhyme replaced alliteration as the usual patterning device of verse in English. Shakespeare's *Sonnets* have every other line rhyming as in "CXXX":

> My mistress' eyes are nothing like the sun;
> Coral is far more red than her lips' red:
> If snow be white, why then her breasts are dun;
> If hairs be wire, black wires grow on her head.
>
> lines 1 – 4

see: *couplet, poetry*

From Milton's *Paradise Lost*

Riddle - a puzzling problem or question, or an enigmatic saying or speech. The term also applies to a statement or query so phrased as to require ingenuity in discovering its meaning.

The term is from the Anglo-Saxon *roedels* derived from *roedan*, meaning "to read."

This literary form existed during Greek and Roman times and the Middle Ages.

In Sophocles's *The Oedipus Trilogy* (line 1524), King Oedipus of Thebes solved the most famous riddle—that of the Sphinx:

> What goes on four feet, on two feet, and three
> But the more feet it goes on, the weaker is he?

The answer is a man, who as an infant crawls upon all fours, as an adult walks erect on his own two feet, and in old age supports his tottering legs with a staff (the third leg).

Saga - a lengthy narrative or legend about heroic or historical events. The term applies particularly to any Scandinavian story from the middle ages dealing with the adventures of a person of lofty rank, but also applies to any traditional legend, myth, or tale involving extraordinary, marvelous, or detailed experiences and achievements. Its emphasis on feuds and family histories led the term to additionally be used to describe a long family story spanning two or more generations.

The term is from the Icelandic *saw*, meaning "saying," and the Old Norse *saga*, meaning "story."

The Forsythe Saga by John Galsworthy is an example of a contemporary saga; *Erik the Red* and *Hrafnkel's Saga* are two examples of traditional Icelandic sagas.

Satire - the use of humor and wit with a critical attitude, irony, sarcasm, or ridicule for exposing or denouncing the frailties and faults of mankind's activities and institutions, such as folly, stupidity, or vice. This usually involves both moral judgment and a desire to help improve a custom, belief, or tradition.

The term is from the Latin *satura,* meaning "full" or "sated" and was derived from *satis,* meaning "enough" or "sufficient."

Satire began with the early Greek poets when they were supposed to tax weaknesses and correct vice. As a distinct literary form, satire was the creation of the Romans and was subsequently present in many forms of medieval literature. In *The Canterbury Tales,* Chaucer used this technique for "The Miller's Tale" and "The Nun's Priest's Tale." During the Renaissance, satire was more often prose rather than poetry. The Golden Age of Satire in England was the early Eighteenth Century when Henry Fielding, Jonathan Swift, Alexander Pope, John Gay and others dominated British letters.

In the Twentieth Century, satire includes George Orwell's *Animal Farm* and *1984* which satirized political situations and the status quo, Aldous Huxley's *Brave New World* which satirized utopian dreams.

see: *lampoon, parody*

Scenario - an outline of the plot of a dramatic work, which provides particulars about characters, settings, and situation. The term is most often used for the detailed script of a film or a treatment setting forth the action in the sequence it is to follow with detailed descriptions of scenes and characters, and actual works. Sometimes the plot of a film or television show is loosely called a scenario.

The term is from the Latin *scena* which was derived from the Greek *skene,* meaning "booth" or "stage."

Scene - the place where some act or event occurs. Sometimes the term is used for an incident or situation in real life. It is also the division of an act of a play or a unit of dramatic action in which a single point is made or one effect obtained.

The etymology of scene is the same as that of scenario discussed above.

Originally, the term meant the stone or wooden background

behind the stage in the ancient Greek or Roman theater; the stage itself was called the proscenium.

Science fiction - a narrative which draws imaginatively on scientific knowledge, theory, speculation, and the effects of future events on human beings in its plot, theme, and setting. It considers these events rationally in terms of explanation and consequences and is concerned with the impact of change on people. This is a form of fantasy which hypothesizes by logical extrapolation about the possibilities of space travel, adventures on other planets, etc. Recently, it has become a form of literature that takes place in an alternative present, a preconceived past, or an extrapolated future with these alterations based upon technological or sociological changes in the present.

Science is from Middle English through Middle French into which it was derived from *scient*, meaning "having knowledge." The etymology of fiction was discussed previously under that term.

Such narratives have existed since the second century when Lucian of Samosata wrote *Vera Historia* in which he created a hero who traveled to the moon and the sun and was involved in interplanetary warfare. Jonathan Swift's 1726 *Gulliver's Travels* was based upon an imaginary voyage. Shelley's 1818 *Frankenstein* is permeated by a belief in the potential of science. Twain's *A Connecticut Yankee in King Arthur's Court* contains time travel. Jules Verne, who authored *Twenty Thousand Leagues Under the Sea*, and H. G. Wells, who authored *The Time Machine*, are considered the modern fathers of the genre. The term was coined by Hugo Gernsback, editor of *Amazing Stories* magazine in the 1920s.

see: *apocalyptic, fantasy*

Semantics - the branch of linguistics that deals with the meanings of words, expressions, and sentences, and with historical changes in those meanings. The term may also be taken to include the relations between signs (words, symbols) and the mental and physical actions called forth by their meanings.

From Sophocles's *The Oedipus Trilogy*

The term is from the Greek *semantikos*, meaning "significant," which was derived from *semainein*, meaning "to show."

Short story - a narrative that is designed to produce a single dominant effect and which contains the elements of drama. It may concentrate on a single character in a single situation at a single moment. Dramatic conflict is at the heart of a short story even if it has more than one of the above elements.

Short comes through Middle English from the Old English *sceort*, meaning "short." Story also comes through Middle English, but from the Old French *estorie* derived from the Latin *historia*, which itself was derived from the Greek *histor*, meaning "knowing" or "learned."

Margaret Cavendish wrote early versions of the short story in the Seventeenth Century. While short stories appear inside some of Defoe's earlier novels, Poe is considered the father of the modern short story, which developed greatly in the Nineteenth Century due to their popularity in magazines.

Some examples of short stories are Kafka's "Metamorphosis" and Henry James's "The Jolly Corner." James Joyce's *Dubliners* (1907) was a breakthrough collection of powerful short stories, including perhaps the most famous short story in English, "The Dead."

Simile - a figure of speech in which two things, essentially different but thought to be alike in one or more respects, are compared using "like," "as," "as if," or "such" for the purpose of explanation, allusion, or ornament.

The term is from the Latin *similis*, meaning "like."

Common contemporary similes are "running like a bat out of hell" and "working nonstop as if possessed." There is a simile in John Milton's *Paradise Lost*:

> Anon out of the earth a Fabrick huge
> Rose like an Exhalation, with the sound

Of Dulcet Symphony and voices sweet.

Book I : lines 710 – 712

Perhaps the best known simile in English poetry is Robert Burns's line:

"My love is like a red, red rose."

see: *allusion, figure of speech, metaphor*

Soliloquy - a speech delivered by a character in a play or other literature while alone, or an utterance by a person who is talking to him/herself, disregardful of or oblivious to any hearers present. This technique is frequently used to disclose a character's innermost feeling, such as thoughts, state of mind, motives, and intentions or to provide information needed by the audience or reader.

The term is from the Late Latin *soliloquium,* coined by St. Augustine, the Bishop of Hippo, from the Greek *monologia* which was derived by combining *solus,* meaning "alone," and *loqui,* meaning "to speak."

Rare in Classical drama, Elizabethan and Jacobean playwrights used it extensively, especially for their villains, as they manipulated the plot and commented on the action, such as in Shakespeare's *Macbeth, Hamlet,* and Iago in *Othello.*

A well-known example is Hamlet's soliloquy which begins with:

O, that this too too sullied flesh would melt,
Thaw, and resolve itself into a dew!
Or that the Everlasting had not fix'd
His canon 'gainst self-slaughter! . . .

Act I, scene ii : lines 129 – 132

see: *device, interior monologue, monologue*

Sonnet - a lyric poem of 14 lines, usually in iambic pentameter, with rhymes arranged according to certain definite patterns. It usually expresses a single, complete thought, idea, or sentiment.

From Huxley's *Brave New World*

There are three different forms: Petrarchan (or Italian), English (or Shakespearean), and Miltonic. The Petrarchan has an eight line stanza (called octave) followed by a six line stanza (called sestet). The octave has two quatrains rhyming abba, abba, the first of which presents the theme, while the second develops it. In the sestet, the first three lines exemplify or reflect on the theme, while the last three bring the poem to a unified end. There are two or three different rhymes in the sestets arranged cdecde, cdcdcd, or cdedce. The Shakespearean sonnet developed as an adaptation to a language less rich in rhymes than Italian. It has three quatrains, each rhymed differently, with a final, independently rhymed couplet that makes an effective, unifying climax to the whole. Its rhyme scheme is abab, cdcd, efef, gg. The Miltonic sonnet dealt not only with love as the Sixteenth Century sonnet did, but also politics, religion, and personal matters. The Miltonic sonnet has the same arrangement in the octave as the Petrarchan sonnet does, but no division is marked between the octave and sestet, the sense running from the eighth into the ninth line. After Milton, there was a decline in the sonnet's popularity in England until the romantic poets revived it in the Nineteenth Century. The sonnet adapted well to Twentieth Century themes and diction.

The term comes from the Italian *sonetto*, which is a diminutive of *suono*, meaning "sound" and was derived from the Latin *sonus*.

The form was developed in Italy during the early Renaissance and introduced to England by Sir Thomas Wyatt and the Earl of Surrey, Henry Howard, in the mid-Sixteenth Century. Sir Phillip Sidney and Edmund Spenser both produced important sonnet sequences in the late-Sixteenth Century.

The most well-known sonnets are those of Shakespeare, who wrote 154.

This is Number 94:

> They that have power to hurt and will do none,
> That do not do the thing they most do show,

Who, moving others, are themselves as stone,
Unmoved, cold, and to temptation slow —
They rightly do inherit Heaven's graces,
And husband Nature's riches from expense;
They are the lords and owners of their faces,
Others but stewards of their excellence.
The summer flow'r is to the summer sweet
Though to itself it only live and die;
But if that flow'r with base infection meet,
The basest weed outbraves his dignity.
For sweetest things turn sourest by their deeds:
Lilies that fester smell far worse than weeds.

see: *couplet*

Spoonerism - a phrase in which two words' initial consonants have been switched deliberately for a humorous effect.

The term comes from Reverend W. A. Spooner (1844 – 1930), Warden of New College, Oxford, who innocently switched the initial consonants of two words in specific phrases. An example is saying "the queer old dean" for the dear old queen.

Stanza - an arrangement of lines of verse in a pattern usually repeated throughout the poem. It has a fixed number of verses or lines, a prevailing kind of meter, and a consistent rhyme scheme. A stanza may form a division of a poem or constitute a selection in its entirety.

The term is from the Latin *stantem*, which was derived from *stare*, meaning "to stand."

Earlier English terms for stanza were "batch," "fit", and "stave."

see: *ballad, haiku, ode*

Story - a narrative, either true or fictional in prose or verse, designed to interest, amuse, or inform listeners or readers. In literature, it is a sequence of imagined events that the reader constructs from the plot, and may include events preceding or postdating what the reader sees on the printed page, since the story may be started *in medias res.*

The etymology of story is discussed under the listing of short story.

Since a story is a narrative, any prose, such as Chopin's *The Awakening,* Haley's *The Autobiography of Malcom X,* and Hurston's *Their Eyes Were Watching God* are all examples of stories.

see: *allegory, ballad, black comedy, comedy, drama, epic, fable, fantasy, farce, fiction, first person narrative, folk tale, legend, literature, melodrama, morality play, myth, narrative, Noh, novel, parable, parody, pastoral, poetry, plot, prose, saga, satire, science fiction, short story, tragedy*

Style - a manner of putting thoughts into words or the characteristic mode of construction and expression in writing and speaking. The term is also used for the characteristics of a literary selection that concern the form of expression rather than the thought conveyed. Style is usually defined by the writer's choice of words, figures of speech, devices, and the shaping of the sentences and paragraphs. Sometimes, styles are classified according to time period or individual writers.

The term is from the Latin *stilus,* meaning "a pointed instrument for writing on waxed tablets" or the way of writing itself.

Assessments of style are more often generalizations than precise descriptions. Milton, for instance, is commonly thought to have written in a very grand style, while Hemingway is said to have written very plainly. This may generally be the case, but both author's work contains examples of other styles.

see: *figures of speech*

Subplot (also called counterplot) - a secondary or minor plot within a play or other literary work which may contrast with the principal plot, highlight it, or be unrelated. It involves characters of lesser importance than those involved in the major plot.

The term is formed by joining the Latin *sub*, meaning "under," with plot, whose etymology is discussed under that listing.

Subplots were very common in Tudor and Jacobean drama.

In Shakespeare's *King Lear*, there is the subplot concerning Gloucester and his sons Edmund and Edgar: Edgar attempts to convince his father of the lie (with Edmund's complete compliance) that Edmund, who is illegitimate, is trying to murder him. This subplot dealing with the father's persecution of one son and the ingratitude of the other is juxtaposed with King Lear's struggles with the villainy of his daughters, Regan and Goneril, and the innocence of his daughter, Cordelia.

see: *plot*

Synopsis - a condensed statement providing a general view of a topic or subject and more often used with fiction than nonfiction. It is a form of abridgment and is closely related in meaning to compendium, resume, and summary.

The term is from the Greek *sunopsis*, which is a combination of *sun*, meaning "with or together," and *opsis*, meaning "a view."

A synopsis of Twain's *Huckleberry Finn* might be as follows: it tells the adventures of a young Midwestern boy who runs away from home with an escaped slave.

Theme - the central and dominating idea in a literary work. A theme may also be a short essay such as a composition. In addition, the term means a message or moral implicit in any work of art.

The term is from the Greek *thema*, meaning "proposition," which was derived from *tithenai*, meaning "to put."

The theme of Euripides's *The Trojan Women* is anguish over the seeming necessity for war; in Shakespeare's *Othello*, the theme is jealousy.

Thesis - a proposition for consideration, especially one to be discussed and proved or disproved, or a dissertation involving
research on a particular subject. A thesis is less general than a
theme. Thesis novels or plays are referred to as those of ideas
that illustrate, develop, and reinforce an attitude or point of
view of their authors. In poetry, the thesis is the unstressed
syllable of a metrical foot.

The term is from the Greek *thesis*, meaning "a placing" or "ar-
ranging."

According to this definition, Harriet Beecher Stowe's *Uncle
Tom's Cabin* may be considered a thesis novel in that it was written
as an anti-slavery work meant to instruct in the evils of slavery.

see: *essay, novel*

Tragedy - a serious play in which the chief figures, by some peculiarity of character, pass through a series of misfortunes leading to the final catastrophe. In contemporary theater, tragedy
often has the evils of society as the cause of this downfall, especially in Theater of the Absurd. In literature, tragedy refers
to any composition with a somber theme carried to a disas-
trous conclusion. Sometimes, the word is used to refer to an
actual calamity, disaster, or fatal event.

The term is from the Greek *tragoidia* formed by combining
tragos, meaning "he-goat," and *oide*, meaning "song." (A *tragoidos*
was a tragic poet and singer; probably called "a goat singer" because he wore goatskins or because a he-goat was the prize in a
competition among *tragoidos*.)

The form was developed by the Greeks from a ritual sacrifice
accompanied by a choral song in honor of Dionysus, the God of
the Fields and Vineyards. There seem to have been no tragedies
written between Seneca (c. 4 B.C. – A.D. 65) and the Middle Ages.
Tragedy was a popular form in Renaissance drama with Marlowe,
Shakespeare, and others producing powerful plays depicting and
pain and adversity of living.

From Haley's *The Autobigraphy of Malcolm X*

In "The Monk's Tale" of his *Canterbury Tales*, Chaucer defines it as:

> Tragedie is to seyn a certeyn storie,
> As olde bookes maken us memorie,
> Of hym that stood in greet prosperitee
> And is yfallen out of heigh degree
> Into myserie, and endeth wrecchedly.
>
> lines 249 – 253

see: *absurd, antagonist, catharsis, comedy, drama, hubris*

Verse - a line of metrical writing, a stanza, or poetry in general. It also means the method by which one metrical line turns into a new line. In addition, the term refers to one of the short sections into which a chapter of the Bible is divided.

The term comes from the Latin *versus*, meaning a "furrow," "a row," "a line," "a metric line," or literally "turning," which was derived from *vertere*, meaning "to turn."

An Introduction to Shakespearean Language

The Life and Work of William Shakespeare

The details of William Shakespeare's life are sketchy, mostly mere surmise based upon court or other clerical records. His parents, John and Mary (Arden), were married about 1557; she was of the landed gentry, and he was a yeoman—a glover and commodities merchant. By 1568, John had risen through the ranks of town government and held the position of high bailiff, which was a position similar to mayor. William, the eldest son and the third of eight children, was born in 1564, probably on April 23, several days before his baptism on April 26 in Stratford-upon-Avon. Shakespeare is also believed to have died on the same date—April 23—in 1616.

It is believed that Shakespeare attended the local grammar school in Stratford where his parents lived, and that he studied primarily Latin, rhetoric, logic, and literature. Shakespeare probably left school at age 15, which was the norm, to take a job, especially since this was the period of his father's financial difficulty. At age 18 (1582), he married Anne Hathaway, a local farmer's daughter who was eight years his senior. Their first daughter (Susanna) was born six months later (1583), and twins Judith and Hamnet were born in 1585.

Shakespeare's life can be divided into three periods: the first 20 years in Stratford, which include his schooling, early marriage, and fatherhood; the next 25 years as an actor and playwright in London; and the last five in retirement in Stratford where he enjoyed moderate wealth gained from his theatrical successes. The years linking the first two periods are marked by a lack of information about Shakespeare, and are often referred to as the "dark years."

At some point during the "dark years," Shakespeare began his career with a London theatrical company, perhaps in 1589, for he was already an actor and playwright of some note by 1592. Shakespeare apparently wrote and acted for numerous theatrical companies, including Pembroke's Men, and Strange's Men, which later became the Chamberlain's Men, with whom he remained for the rest of his career.

In 1592, the Plague closed the theaters for about two years, and Shakespeare turned to writing book-length narrative poetry. Most notable were *Venus and Adonis* and *The Rape of Lucrece*, both of which were dedicated to the Earl of Southampton, whom scholars accept as Shakespeare's friend and benefactor despite a lack of documentation. During this same period, Shakespeare was writing his sonnets, which are more likely signs of the time's fashion rather than actual love poems detailing any particular relationship. He returned to playwriting when theaters reopened in 1594, and did not continue to write poetry. His sonnets were published without his consent in 1609, shortly before his retirement.

Amid all of his success, Shakespeare suffered the loss of his only son, Hamnet, who died in 1596 at the age of 11. But Shakespeare's career continued unabated, and in London in 1599, he became one of the partners in the new Globe Theater, which was built by the Chamberlain's Men.

Shakespeare wrote very little after 1612, which was the year he completed *Henry VIII*. It was during a performance of this play in 1613 that the Globe caught fire and burned to the ground. Sometime between 1610 and 1613, Shakespeare returned to Stratford, where he owned a large house and property, to spend his remaining years with his family.

William Shakespeare died on April 23, 1616, and was buried two days later in the chancel of Holy Trinity Church, where he had been baptized exactly 52 years earlier. His literary legacy included 37 plays, 154 sonnets, and five major poems.

Incredibly, most of Shakespeare's plays had never been published in anything except pamphlet form, and were simply extant as acting scripts stored at the Globe. Theater scripts were not regarded as literary works of art, but only the basis for the performance. Plays were simply a popular form of entertainment for all layers of society in Shakespeare's time. Only the efforts of two of Shakespeare's company, John Heminges and Henry Condell, preserved his 36 plays (minus *Pericles*, the thirty-seventh).

Shakespeare's Language

Shakespeare's language can create a strong pang of intimidation, even fear, in a large number of modern-day readers. Fortunately, however, this need not be the case. All that is needed to master the art of reading Shakespeare is to practice the techniques of unraveling uncommonly structured sentences and to become familiar with the poetic use of uncommon words. We must realize that during the 400-year span between Shakespeare's time and our own, both the way we live and speak has changed. Although most of his vocabulary is in use today, some of it is obsolete, and what may be most confusing is that some of his words are used today, but with slightly different or totally different meanings. On the stage, actors readily dissolve these language stumbling blocks. They study Shakespeare's dialogue and express it dramatically in word and in action so that its meaning is graphically enacted. If the reader studies Shakespeare's lines as an actor does, looking up and reflecting upon the meaning of unfamiliar words until the real voice is discovered, he or she will suddenly experience the excitement, the depth, and the sheer poetry of what these characters say.

Shakespeare's Sentences

In English, or any other language, the meaning of a sentence greatly depends upon where each word is placed in that sentence.

"The child hurt the mother" and "The mother hurt the child" have opposite meanings, even though the words are the same, simply because the words are arranged differently. Because word position is so integral to English, the reader will find unfamiliar word arrangements confusing, even difficult to understand. Since Shakespeare's plays are poetic dramas, he often shifts from average word arrangements to the strikingly unusual so that the line will conform to the desired poetic rhythm. Often, too, Shakespeare employs unusual word order to afford a character his own specific style of speaking.

Today, English sentence structure follows a sequence of subject first, verb second, and an optional object third. Shakespeare, however, often places the verb before the subject, which reads, "Speaks he" rather than "He speaks." Solanio speaks with this inverted structure in *The Merchant of Venice* stating, "I should be still/Plucking the grass to know where sits the wind" (Bevington edition, I, i, ll. 17–19), while today's standard English word order would have the clause at the end of this line read, "where the wind sits." "Wind" is the subject of this clause, and "sits" is the verb. Bassanio's words in Act Two also exemplify this inversion: "And in such eyes as ours appear not faults" (II, ii, l. 184). In our normal word order, we would say, "Faults do not appear in eyes such as ours," with "faults" as the subject in both Shakespeare's word order and ours.

Inversions like these are not troublesome, but when Shakespeare positions the predicate adjective or the object before the subject and verb, we are sometimes surprised. For example, rather than "I saw him," Shakespeare may use a structure such as "Him I saw." Similarly, "Cold the morning is" would be used for our "The morning is cold." Lady Macbeth demonstrates this inversion as she speaks of her husband: "Glamis thou art, and Cawdor, and shalt be/What thou art promised" (*Macbeth*, I, v, ll. 14 – 15). In current English word order, this quote would begin, "Thou art Glamis, and Cawdor."

In addition to inversions, Shakespeare purposefully keeps words apart that we generally keep together. To illustrate, consider Bassanio's humble admission in *The Merchant of Venice*: "I owe you much, and, like a wilful youth, /That which I owe is lost" (I, i, ll. 146 – 147). The phrase, "like a wilful youth," separates the regular sequence of "I owe you much" and "That which I owe is lost." To understand more clearly this type of passage, the reader could re-arrange these word groups into our conventional order: I owe you much and I wasted what you gave me because I was young and impulsive. While these rearranged clauses will sound like normal English, and will be simpler to understand, they will no longer have the desired poetic rhythm, and the emphasis will now be on the wrong words.

As we read Shakespeare, we will find words that are separated by long, interruptive statements. Often subjects are separated from verbs, and verbs are separated from objects. These long interruptions can be used to give a character dimension or to add an element of suspense. For example, in *Romeo and Juliet*, Benvolio describes both Romeo's moodiness and his own sensitive and thoughtful nature:

> I, measuring his affections by my own,
> Which then most sought, where most might not be found,
> Being one too many by my weary self,
> Pursu'd my humour, not pursuing his,
> And gladly shunn'd who gladly fled from me.
>
> Act I, scene i: lines 126 – 130

In this passage, the subject "I" is distanced from its verb "Pursu'd." The long interruption serves to provide information which is integral to the plot. Another example, taken from *Hamlet*, is the ghost, Hamlet's father, who describes Hamlet's uncle, Claudius, as

> . . . that incestuous, that adulterate beast,
> With witchcraft of his wit, with traitorous gifts—
> O wicked wit and gifts, that have the power
> So to seduce—won to his shameful lust
> The will of my most seeming virtuous queen.
>
> Act I, scene v: lines 43 – 47

From this we learn that Prince Hamlet's mother is the victim of an evil seduction and deception. The delay between the subject, "beast," and the verb, "won," creates a moment of tension filled with the image of a cunning predator waiting for the right moment to spring into attack. This interruptive passage allows the play to unfold crucial information and thus to build the tension necessary to produce a riveting drama.

While at times these long delays are merely for decorative purposes, they are often used to narrate a particular situation or to enhance character development. As *Antony and Cleopatra* opens, an interruptive passage occurs in the first few lines. Although the delay is not lengthy, Philo's words vividly portray Antony's military prowess while they also reveal the immediate concern of the drama. Antony is distracted from his career and is now focused on Cleopatra:

> . . . those goodly eyes,
> That o'er the files and musters of the war
> Have glow'd like plated Mars, now bend, now turn
> The office and devotion of their view
> Upon a tawny front . . . .
>
> Act I, scene i: lines 2 – 6

Whereas Shakespeare sometimes heaps detail upon detail, his sentences are often elliptical, that is, they omit words we expect in written English sentences. In fact, we often do this in our spoken conversations. For instance, we say, "You see that?" when we really mean, "Did you see that?" Reading poetry or listening to lyrics in music conditions us to supply the omitted words and it makes us more comfortable reading this type of dialogue. Consider one passage in *The Merchant of Venice* where Antonio's friends ask him why he seems so sad and Solanio tells Antonio, "Why, then you are in love" (I, i, l. 46). When Antonio denies this, Solanio responds, "Not in love neither?" (I, i, l. 47). The word "you" is omitted but understood despite the confusing double negative.

In addition to leaving out words, Shakespeare often uses intentionally vague language, a strategy which taxes the reader's attentiveness. In *Antony and Cleopatra*, Cleopatra, upset that Antony is leaving for Rome after learning that his wife died in battle, convinces him to stay in Egypt:

> Sir, you and I must part, but that's not it:
> Sir you and I have lov'd, but there's not it;
> That you know well, something it is I would—
> O, my oblivion is a very Antony,
> And I am all forgotten.
>
> Act I, scene iii: lines 87 – 91

In line 89, " . . . something it is I would" suggests that there is something that she would want to say, do, or have done. The intentional vagueness leaves us, and certainly Antony, to wonder. Though this sort of writing may appear lackadaisical for all that it leaves out, here the vagueness functions to portray Cleopatra as rhetorically sophisticated. Similarly, when asked what thing a crocodile is (meaning Antony himself who is being compared to a crocodile), Antony slyly evades the question by giving a vague reply:

> It is shap'd, sir, like itself, and it is as broad as it hath
> breadth. It is just so high as it is, and moves with it own
> organs. It lives by that which nourisheth it, and, the
> elements once out of it, it transmigrates.
>
> Act II, scene vii, lines 43 – 46

This kind of evasiveness, or double-talk, occurs often in Shakespeare's writing and requires extra patience on the part of the reader.

Shakespeare's Words

As we read Shakespeare's plays, we will encounter uncommon words. Many of these words are not in use today. As *Romeo and Juliet* opens, we notice words like "shrift" (confession) and "holidame" (a holy relic). Words like these should be explained in notes to the text. Shakespeare also employs words which we still use, though with different meaning. For example, in *The Merchant of Venice*, "caskets" refer to small, decorative chests for holding jewels. However, modern readers may think of a large cask instead of the smaller, diminutive casket.

Another trouble modern readers will have with Shakespeare's English is with words that are still in use today, but which mean something different in Elizabethan use. In *The Merchant of Venice*, Shakespeare uses the word "straight" (as in "straight away") where we would say "immediately." Here, the modern reader is unlikely to carry away the wrong message, however, since the modern meaning will simply make no sense. In this case, textual notes will clarify a phrase's meaning. To cite another example, in *Romeo and Juliet*, after Mercutio dies, Romeo states that the "black fate on moe days doth depend." In this case, "depend" really means "impend."

Shakespeare's Wordplay

All of Shakespeare's works exhibit his mastery of playing with language and with such variety that many people have authored entire books on this subject alone. Shakespeare's most frequently used types of wordplay are common: metaphors, similes, synecdoche and metonymy, personification, allusion, and puns. It is when Shakespeare violates the normal use of these devices, or rhetorical figures, that the language becomes confusing.

A metaphor is a comparison in which an object or idea is replaced by another object or idea with common attributes. For example, in *Macbeth*, a murderer tells Macbeth that Banquo has been murdered, as directed, but that his son, Fleance, escaped, having witnessed his father's murder. Fleance, now a threat to Macbeth, is described as a serpent:

> There the grown serpent lies, the worm that's fled
> Hath nature that in time will venom breed,
> No teeth for the present.

Act III, scene iv: lines 29 – 31

Similes, on the other hand, compare objects or ideas while using the words "like" or "as." In *Romeo and Juliet*, Romeo tells Juliet that "Love goes toward love as schoolboys from their books" (II, ii, l. 156). Such similes often give way to more involved comparisons, "extended similes." For example, Juliet tells Romeo:

> 'Tis almost morning, I would have thee gone,
> And yet no farther than a wanton's bird,
> That lets it hop a little from his hand
> Like a poor prisoner in his twisted gyves,
> And with silken thread plucks it back again,
> So loving-jealous of his liberty.
>
> > Act II, scene ii: lines 176 – 181

An epic simile, a device borrowed from heroic poetry, is an extended simile that builds into an even more elaborate comparison. In *Macbeth*, Macbeth describes King Duncan's virtues with an angelic, celestial simile and then drives immediately into another simile that redirects us into a vision of warfare and destruction:

> > ... Besides this Duncan
> Hath borne his faculties so meek, hath been
> So clear in his great office, that his virtues
> Will plead like angels, trumpet-tongued, against
> The deep damnation of his taking-off;
> And pity, like a naked new-born babe,
> Striding the blast, or heaven's cherubim, horsed
> Upon the sightless couriers of the air,
> Shall blow the horrid deed in every eye,
> That tears shall drown the wind....
>
> > Act I, scene vii: lines 16 – 25

Shakespeare employs other devices, like synecdoche and metonymy, to achieve "verbal economy," or using one or two words to express more than one thought. Synecdoche is a figure of speech using a part for the whole. An example of synecdoche is using the word boards to imply a stage. Boards are only a small part of the materials that make up a stage; however, the term boards has become a colloquial synonym for stage. Metonymy is a figure of speech using the name of one thing for that of another with which it is associated. An example of metonymy is using crown to mean the king (as used in the sentence "These lands belong to the crown"). Since a crown is associated with or an attribute of the king, the word crown has become a metonymy for the king. It is important to understand that every metonymy is a synecdoche, but not every synecdoche is a metonymy. This rule is true because a metonymy must not only be a part of the root word, making a synecdoche, but also be a unique attribute of or associated with the root word.

Synecdoche and metonymy in Shakespeare's works are often very confusing to a new student because he creates uses for words that they usually do not perform. This technique is often complicated and yet very subtle, which makes it difficult for a new student to dissect and understand. An example of these devices in one of Shakespeare's plays can be found in *The Merchant of Venice*. In warning his daughter, Jessica, to ignore the Christian revelries in the streets below, Shylock says:

> Lock up my doors; and when you hear the drum
> And the vile squealing of the wry-necked fife,
> Clamber not you up to the casements then . . .
>
> Act II, scene v: lines 29-31

The phrase of importance in this passage is "the wry-necked fife." When a reader examines this phrase, it does not seem to make sense; a fife is a cylinder-shaped instrument, there is no part of it that can be called a neck. The phrase then must be taken to refer to the fife-player, who has to twist his or her neck to play the fife. Fife, therefore, is metonymic for fife-player, much as "crown" is for "king". The trouble with understanding this phrase is that "vile squealing" logically refers to the sound of the fife, not the fife-player, and the reader might be led to take fife as the instrument because of the parallel reference to "drum" in the previous line. The best solution to this quandary is that Shakespeare uses the word fife to refer to both the instrument and the player. Both the player and the instrument are needed to complete the wordplay in this phrase, which, though difficult to understand to new readers, cannot be seen as a flaw since Shakespeare manages to convey two meanings with one word. This remarkable example of metonymy illuminates Shakespeare's mastery of "verbal economy."

Shakespeare also uses vivid and imagistic wordplay through personification, in which human capacities and behaviors are attributed to inanimate objects. Bassanio, in *The Merchant of Venice*, almost speechless when Portia promises to marry him and share all her worldly wealth, states "my blood speaks to you in my veins . . ." (III, ii, l. 176). Similarly, Portia, learning of the penalty that Antonio must pay for defaulting on his debt, tells Salerio, "There are some shrewd contents in yond same paper/That steals the color from Bassanio's cheek" (III, ii, ll. 243 – 244).

Another important facet of Shakespeare's rhetorical repertoire is his use of allusion. An allusion is a reference to another author or to a historical figure or event. Very often Shakespeare alludes to the heroes and heroines of Ovid's *Metamorphoses*. For example, in Cymbeline an entire room is decorated with images illustrating the stories from this classical work, and the heroine, Imogen, has been reading from this text. Similarly, in *Titus Andronicus*, characters not only read directly from the *Metamorphoses*, but a subplot re-enacts one of the *Metamorphoses's* most famous stories, the rape and mutilation of Philomel.

Another way Shakespeare uses allusion is to drop names of mythological, historical, and literary figures. In *The Taming of the Shrew*, for instance, Petruchio compares Katharina, the woman whom he is courting, to Diana (II, i, l. 55), the virgin goddess, in order to suggest that Katharina is a man-hater. At times, Shakespeare will allude to well-known figures without so much as mentioning their names. In *Twelfth Night*, for example, though the Duke and Valentine are ostensibly interested in Olivia, a rich countess, Shakespeare asks his audience to compare the Duke's emotional turmoil to the plight of Acteon, whom the goddess Diana transforms into a deer to be hunted and killed by Acteon's own dogs:

Duke: That instant was I turn'd into a hart,
                 And my desires, like fell and cruel hounds,
                 E'er since pursue me.
                 [...]

Valentine: But like a cloistress she will veiled walk,
              And water once a day her chamber round . . . .
                                          Act I, scene i: line 20 ff.

Shakespeare's use of puns spotlights his exceptional wit. His comedies in particular are loaded with puns, usually of a sexual nature. Puns work through the ambiguity that results when multiple senses of a word are evoked; homophones often cause this sort of ambiguity. In *Antony and Cleopatra*, Enobarbus believes "there is mettle in death" (I, ii, l. 146), meaning that there is "courage" in death; at the same time, mettle suggests the homophone metal, referring to swords made of metal causing death. In early editions of Shakespeare's work there was no distinction made between the two words. Antony puns on the word "earing" (I, ii, ll. 112 – 114), meaning both plowing (as in rooting out weeds) and hearing: he angrily sends away a messenger, not wishing to hear the message from his wife, Fulvia: ". . . O then we bring forth weeds,/ when our quick minds lie still, and our ills told us/Is as our earing." If ill-natured news is planted in one's "hearing," it will render an "earing" (harvest) of ill-natured thoughts. A particularly clever pun, also in *Antony and Cleopatra,* stands out after Antony's troops have fought Octavius's men in Egypt: "We have beat him to his camp. Run one before,/And let the queen know of our gests" (IV, viii, ll. 1 – 2). Here "gests" means deeds (in this case, deeds of battle); it is also a pun on "guests," as though Octavius's slain soldiers were to be guests when buried in Egypt.

One should note that Elizabethan pronunciation was in several cases different from our own. Thus, modern readers, especially Americans, will miss out on the many puns based on homophones. The textual notes will point out many of these "lost" puns, however.

Shakespeare's sexual innuendoes can be either clever or tedious depending upon the speaker and situation. The modern reader should recall that sexuality in Shakespeare's time was far more complex than in ours and that characters may refer to such things as masturbation and homosexual activity. Textual notes in some editions will point out these puns but rarely explain them. An example of a sexual pun or innuendo can be found in *The Mer-*

chant of Venice when Portia and Nerissa are discussing Portia's past suitors using innuendo to tell of their sexual prowess:

> Portia: I pray thee, overname them, and as thou namest them, I will describe them, and according to my description level at my affection.
>
> Nerissa: First, there is the Neapolitan prince.
>
> Portia: Ay, that's a colt indeed, for he doth nothing but talk of his horse, and he makes it a great appropriation to his own good parts that he can shoe him himself. I am much afeard my lady his mother played false with the smith.
>
> Act I, scene ii: lines 35 – 45

The "Neapolitan prince" is given a grade of an inexperienced youth when Portia describes him as a "colt." The prince is thought to be inexperienced because he did nothing but "talk of his horse" (a pun for his penis) and his other great attributes. Portia goes on to say that the prince boasted that he could "shoe him [his horse] himself," a possible pun meaning that the prince was very proud that he could masturbate. Finally, Portia makes an attack upon the prince's mother, saying that "my lady his mother played false with the smith," a pun to say his mother must have committed adultery with a blacksmith to give birth to such a vulgar man having an obsession with "shoeing his horse."

It is worth mentioning that Shakespeare gives the reader hints when his characters might be using puns and innuendoes. In *The Merchant of Venice*, Portia's lines are given in prose when she is joking, or engaged in bawdy conversations. Later on the reader will notice that Portia's lines are rhymed in poetry, such as when she is talking in court or to Bassanio. This is Shakespeare's way of letting the reader know when Portia is jesting and when she is serious.

Shakespeare's Dramatic Verse

Finally, the reader will notice that some lines are actually rhymed verse while others are in verse without rhyme; and much of Shakespeare's drama is in prose. Shakespeare usually has his lovers speak in the language of love poetry which uses rhymed couplets. The archetypal example of this comes, of course, from *Romeo and Juliet*:

> The grey-ey'd morn smiles on the frowning night,
> Check'ring the eastern clouds with streaks of light,
> And fleckled darkness like a drunkard reels
> From forth day's path and Titan's fiery wheels.
>
> > Act II, scene iii: lines 1 – 4

Here it is ironic that Friar Lawrence should speak these lines since he is not the one in love. He, therefore, appears buffoonish and out of touch with reality. Shakespeare often has his characters speak in rhymed verse to let the reader know that the character is acting in jest, and vice-versa.

Perhaps the majority of Shakespeare's lines are in blank verse, a form of poetry which does not use rhyme (hence the name blank) but still employs a rhythm native to the English language, iambic pentameter, where every second syllable in a line of ten syllables receives stress. Consider the following verses from *Hamlet*, and note the accents and the lack of end-rhyme:

> The síngle ánd pecúliar lífe is bóund
> With áll the stréngth and ármor óf the mínd
>
> > Act III, scene iii: lines 12 – 13

The final syllable of these verses receives stress and is said to have a hard, or "strong," ending. A soft ending, also said to be "weak," receives no stress. In *The Tempest*, Shakespeare uses a soft ending to shape a verse that demonstrates through both sound (meter) and sense the capacity of the feminine to propagate:

> and thén I lóv'd thee
> And shów'd thee áll the quálitíes o' th' ísle,
> The frésh spríngs, bríne-pits, bárren pláce and fértile.
>
> > Act I, scene ii: lines 338 – 40

The first and third lines here have soft endings.

In general, Shakespeare saves blank verse for his characters of noble birth. Therefore, it is significant when his lofty characters speak in prose. Prose holds a special place in Shakespeare's dialogues; he uses it to represent the speech habits of the common people. Not only do lowly servants and common citizens speak in prose, but important, lower class figures also use this fun, at times ribald, variety of speech. Though Shakespeare crafts some very ornate lines in verse, his prose can be equally daunting, for some of his characters may speechify and break into double-talk in their attempts to show sophistication. A clever instance of this comes when the Third Citizen in *Coriolanus* refers to the people's paradoxical lack of power when they must elect Coriolanus as their new leader once Coriolanus has orated how he has courageously fought for them in battle:

> We have power in ourselves to do it, but it is a power that we have no power to do; for if he show us his wounds and tell us his deeds, we are to put our tongues into those wounds and speak for them; so, if he tell us his noble deeds, we must also tell him our noble acceptance of them. Ingratitude is monstrous, and for the multitude to be ingrateful were to make a monster of the multitude, of the which we, being members, should bring ourselves to be monstrous members.
>
> Act II, scene ii: lines 3 – 13

Notice that this passage contains as many metaphors, hideous though they be, as any other passage in Shakespeare's dramatic verse.

When reading Shakespeare, paying attention to characters who suddenly break into rhymed verse, or who slip into prose after speaking in blank verse, will heighten your awareness of a character's mood and personal development. For instance, in *Antony and Cleopatra*, the famous military leader Marcus Antony usually speaks in blank verse, but also speaks in fits of prose (II, iii, ll. 43 – 46) once his masculinity and authority have been questioned. Similarly, in *Timon of Athens*, after the wealthy Lord Timon abandons the city of Athens to live in a cave, he harangues anyone whom he encounters in prose (IV, iii, l. 331 ff.). In contrast, the reader should wonder why the bestial Caliban in *The Tempest* speaks in blank verse rather than in prose.

Implied Stage Action

When we read a Shakespearean play, we are reading a performance text. Actors interact through dialogue, but at the same time these actors cry, gesticulate, throw tantrums, pick up daggers, and compulsively wash murderous "blood" from their hands. Some of the action that takes place on stage is explicitly stated in stage directions. However, some of the stage activity is couched within the dialogue itself. Attentiveness to these cues is important as one conceives how to visualize the action. When Iago in *Othello* feigns concern for Cassio whom he himself has stabbed, he calls to the surrounding men, "Come, come:/Lend me a light" (V, i, ll. 86 – 87). It is almost sure that one of the actors involved will bring him a torch or lantern. In the same play, Emilia, Desdemona's maidservant, asks if she should fetch her lady's nightgown and Desdemona replies, "No, unpin me here" (IV, iii, l. 37). In *Macbeth*, after killing Duncan, Macbeth brings the murder weapon back with him. When he tells his wife that he cannot return to the scene and place the daggers to suggest that the king's guards murdered Duncan, she castigates him: "Infirm of purpose/Give me the daggers. The sleeping and the dead are but as pictures" (II, ii, ll. 50 – 52). As she exits, it is easy to visualize Lady Macbeth grabbing the daggers from her husband.

For 400 years, readers have found it greatly satisfying to work with all aspects of Shakespeare's language—the implied stage action, word choice, sentence structure, and wordplay—until all aspects come to life. Just as seeing a fine performance of a Shakespearean play is exciting, staging the play in one's own mind, and revisiting lines to enrich the sense of the action, will enhance one's appreciation of Shakespeare's extraordinary literary and dramatic achievements.

MAXnotes®

REA's Literature Study Guides

MAXnotes® are student-friendly. They offer a fresh look at masterpieces of literature, presented in a lively and interesting fashion. **MAXnotes®** offer the essentials of what you should know about the work, including outlines, explanations and discussions of the plot, character lists, analyses, and historical context. **MAXnotes®** are designed to help you think independently about literary works by raising various issues and thought-provoking ideas and questions. Written by literary experts who currently teach the subject, **MAXnotes®** enhance your understanding and enjoyment of the work.

Available **MAXnotes®** include the following:

Absalom, Absalom!
The Aeneid of Virgil
Animal Farm
Antony and Cleopatra
As I Lay Dying
As You Like It
The Autobiography of
    Malcolm X
The Awakening
Beloved
Beowulf
Billy Budd
The Bluest Eye, A Novel
Brave New World
The Canterbury Tales
The Catcher in the Rye
The Color Purple
The Crucible
Death in Venice
Death of a Salesman
The Divine Comedy I: Inferno
Dubliners
Emma
Euripides' Medea & Electra
Frankenstein
Gone with the Wind
The Grapes of Wrath
Great Expectations
The Great Gatsby
Gulliver's Travels
Hamlet
Hard Times

Heart of Darkness
Henry IV, Part I
Henry V
The House on Mango Street
Huckleberry Finn
I Know Why the Caged
    Bird Sings
The Iliad
Invisible Man
Jane Eyre
Jazz
The Joy Luck Club
Jude the Obscure
Julius Caesar
King Lear
Les Misérables
Lord of the Flies
Macbeth
The Merchant of Venice
Metamorphoses of Ovid
Metamorphosis
Middlemarch
A Midsummer Night's Dream
Moby-Dick
Moll Flanders
Mrs. Dalloway
Much Ado About Nothing
My Antonia
Native Son
1984
The Odyssey
Oedipus Trilogy

Of Mice and Men
On the Road
Othello
Paradise Lost
A Passage to India
Plato's Republic
Portrait of a Lady
A Portrait of the Artist
    as a Young Man
Pride and Prejudice
A Raisin in the Sun
Richard II
Romeo and Juliet
The Scarlet Letter
Sir Gawain and the
    Green Knight
Slaughterhouse-Five
Song of Solomon
The Sound and the Fury
The Stranger
The Sun Also Rises
A Tale of Two Cities
The Taming of the Shrew
The Tempest
Tess of the D'Urbervilles
Their Eyes Were Watching God
To Kill a Mockingbird
To the Lighthouse
Twelfth Night
Uncle Tom's Cabin
Waiting for Godot
Wuthering Heights

THE BEST TEST PREPARATION FOR THE

SAT II: Subject Test

WRITING

by the Staff of Research & Education Association

6 Full-Length Exams

➤ Every question based on the current exams
➤ The ONLY test preparation book with detailed explanations to every question
➤ Far more comprehensive than any other test preparation book

Includes a Comprehensive COURSE REVIEW of Writing, emphasizing all major topics found on the exam

R&EA *Research & Education Association*

Available at your local bookstore or order directly from us by sending in coupon below.

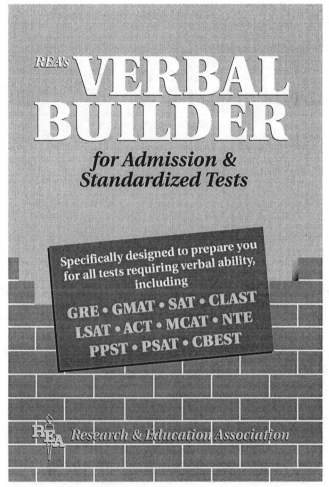

Available at your local bookstore or order directly from us by sending in coupon below.